MUSINGS

MUSINGS

N. JOHN HALL

For David & Jean

love

Jack

NEW YORK

2021

10/20/21

Musings

Copyright © 2021 by N. John Hall

All rights reserved. No part of this book may be reproduced or transmitted in any form or by any means without written permission from the author.

ISBN: 978-0-578-25608-5

These essays originally appeared as blogs, "Musings of an Honorary Alte Kaker" (njohnhall.wordpress.com), from January through August 2021. One of them is a memorial tribute to my colleague Gerhard Joseph (1931-2021). Some passages draw on *Belief: A Memoir* (2007) and are included with the permission of the publisher, Frederic C. Beil.

Cover photograph by Thomas Studios, Newark NJ. The sitter seems, even at age four or five, to be musing.

For Julia Miele Rodas

CONTENTS

To Blog?   1

Chance   5

English As She Is Spoken   9

What's Your Name?   11

In The Bronx   15

On Not Learning Greek   19

Sydney Smith's Home Remedy   25

A Painful Case   29

Fire   31

Ashes   35

Paradise   39

Of Course   45

A Reluctance   49

A Man Called Like   53

La Bohème   57

Waiting On Line   61

A Tontine   63

A Nasty Rant   67

You Call This Fun?   69

Customer Service   73

Wine Anyone?   75

Gerhard Joseph   79

Vaccine Ridiculousness   89

Long Ago   93

Just The Book For You   97

Some Blessedly Brief Words On Spirituality   101

The GC   105

The Enormity Of It All   111

Black And White In The Bronx   115

Come, My Agnostic Friends   119

Goddam Right   125

Comedy: An Apologia   131

Clichés   137

The Church & Sexual Sin: Part I   143

The Church & Sexual Sin: Part II   151

Viva San Fermín   159

Child Abuse   167

Metaphor Everywhere   173

NOTE

These musings grew out of the isolation occasioned by the Covid19 Pandemic, the garrulousness of old age (88), and the encouragement of my dear friend and former student, to whom I dedicate this collection. Musings are allied to essays, and essays are by their nature personal and limited; accordingly, mine make no claim to careful research. Rather, as in the seldom-used verb form of the word essay, they attempt to offer modest thoughts on a variety of subjects, some of them lighthearted and some very serious. But all of them emerge from the context of a pandemic-induced crisis, with its looming threat of illness and death. In such dark circumstances, my wish in these essays is to offer a light note, some playful surcease.

The inescapable fact that essays are autobiographical calls to my mind the words of a character in Joyce who says to his fellow oldsters: "Thanks be to God that we have lived so long and did so little harm." If this non-believer may borrow from those sentiments, I print these reflections in the hope that they too will do little harm and even some possible good.

NJH

TO BLOG?

SOMETIME LAST year I sent an email to relatives and friends, saying that while youngsters—anyone under 65—may be busy working from home, others of us, older folks, may be feeling bored and unproductive. So I passed along the only line I can recall from Montaigne's *Essays*: he writes that when he hears a person lament having "done nothing today," he replies, "What? Have you not lived?" Then, two days later, Julia Miele Rodas, who had taken courses with me in the PhD English program at the CUNY Graduate Center in the 1990s, called on the phone and told me that I was bored and had better get back to writing. I answered that I felt written out, that I had no project or subject. She countered that I should write essays, light-hearted ones. She would set me up with a blog. I didn't have a firm idea of just what a blog was. Moreover, I disliked the word. "OK. Consider them essays," she said. So here goes, with thanks to Julia.

Where to start? (Ah, Bunny Berigan's version of "I Can't Get Started"; radio listeners to the Make-Believe Ballroom on WNEW in 1950 voted it the most requested recording of the first half of 20th century—just most requested, not the most sold, which distinction went to Bing Crosby's "White Christmas"). And there you see immediately a problem, my tendency to run off into asides, digressions, parentheses, and even to put them in the worst place, namely, at the beginning. So I'll start again. To blog or not? I could just say, *It's something to do*, and leave it at that. Of course, there are other reasons to write: to be published, to be admired, to make money, to advance one's career, to unleash some public revelation. None of these apply to me. But I will mention that I take inspiration from Max Beerbohm, because these "blogs" are essays, and he was the foremost essayist of his time. How can I say that? I call to witness Virginia Woolf:

> What Mr Beerbohm gave [in his essays] was, of course, himself.... He was affected by private joys and sorrows, and had no gospel to preach, and no learning to impart. He was himself, simply and directly, and himself he has remained.... He brought personality into literature, not unconsciously and impurely, but so consciously and purely that we do not know whether there is any relation between Max the essayist and Mr Beerbohm the man. We know only that the spirit of personality permeates every word he writes. The triumph is the triumph of style.

Considering these words and others she wrote, namely that Max is "the prince of essayists," and that she "cannot imagine what it would be like to be write as he does," I think we should sit up and take notice. And I cannot resist quoting this modest prince himself when he says that he had no writerly ambitions, that his hope was "to make good use of such little talents as [he] had ... to pass muster." He also said that in writing, "Good sense about trivialities is better than nonsense about things that matter," and that some people are born "to lift heavy weights," while others, like himself, are born "to juggle golden balls." So, I hope herein—for the most part—to hazard what I hope to be some "sense about trivialities" rather than nonsense about important things. Now, to be clear, I have no illusions: I am no closer to being Max Beerbohm than I am to being Montaigne or

Charles Lamb or Dr Johnson. But, while I am not even trying to imitate Max, I do take inspiration, hope, and example from him. That's all. You may well ask, do I have any qualifications other than my admiration for an accomplished master? Surely one needs more than that? Well, I do have an interest in facts (and, I suppose, factoids), facts unrelated, random, and unimportant, but still facts. Such as, did you know that it takes eight minutes for light from the sun to reach the Earth but four years for light from the nearest other star to reach us? Or that Gabriel Garcia Marquez decided as a young man never in his writing to use *mente* adverbs, "ly" adverbs like *felizmente*, happily? So, I have an interest in facticity. (It's a word John Updike is fond of, and in a way the foundation of his fiction.) Then too, some friends tell me that amusing lines and anecdotes have a way of staying with me. I don't know, but I can hope it's true. So, why write? As I just said, in italics no less, it's something to do. Moreover, I'll try to do better next time and to bear in mind Max Beerbohm's point that "It's harder to write bad prose than to write bad poetry."

CHANCE

JUST BACK FROM a walk around the block (farther than it sounds: the distance between Fifth and Sixth Avenues is three blocks, so a walk around my block here on West 10th Street is eight blocks). About halfway around, bundled up and leaning on my cane, I was accosted by someone who asked for 50 cents. In the cold and wind, I wanted to keep moving, and simply said, "I'm sorry," and went on. Then I regretted I had not helped him. Coming full circle and about to enter my building, I decided on the spur of the moment that I should get more exercise by walking back to Sixth Avenue. Then the same homeless person, having circled the block counterclockwise, overtook me (I don't move fast these days) and asked again for 50 cents, or anything, even a quarter. I took off my gloves to extricate my wallet, hoping it contained a single—what if I had only a five, or a ten? Could he make change? But there was a one-dollar bill, and we parted contented, I probably more than he.

Different thoughts came to me as I returned here to my apartment and to my desk: A dollar would not do much to relieve him. Was he a fake? I don't think so, and besides, what did that matter?

Then there came to mind an episode from my days as a priest in Netcong, NJ. It was at the dinner table, and I announced that I had been reading a book on mental illnesses that explained how most beggars were sick rather than lazy or dishonest. A visiting priest, an itinerant "missionary" (who took advantage of my kind elderly pastor by showing up continually for special duties, masses, missions, etc, all of which paid him money) went into a tantrum, screaming denunciations at me and the very idea. I fear that many today hold by the same barbaric notion of mental illness.

My next thought was that we should live in a country where the state, with our tax money, takes care of sick individuals.

I also thought of my dear little granddaughter, Elaina. I have known her since the day of her birth, so to me she is always "little Elaina" although she is now 13. Elaina was taken from her neglectful mother seven years ago and given into the care of her aunt Toni, a single woman who has literally devoted her life to bringing up her niece. The two of them came to mind because of the way Toni handles situations such as mine with a beggar. When she and Elaina see some homeless person with a cup, Toni gives Elaina a dollar and has her go up to the unfortunate man—or, these days, frequently an unfortunate woman—and hand over the dollar. Talk about child rearing.

But what came to my mind most forcefully were my frequent animadversions on luck, chance. Here was a very small chance with a small outcome, namely the chance that resulted in my not entering the building as I had intended, that unplanned little turning that had solaced my mild sense of guilt. Inconsequential, of course. But events like this one usually end with my mind ascending to the frightening thought that everything, or rather almost everything, happens by chance. I won't go into it further here, won't start quoting various authorities. Instead, I'll settle for a single passage from the Bible, no less, a passage from the one book in the whole thing that really gets to me, Ecclesiastes 9:11 (what?) rendered thus in the great King James Version:

I returned, and saw under the sun, that the race is not to the swift, nor the battle to the strong, neither yet bread to the wise, nor yet riches to men of understanding, nor yet favour to men of skill; but time and chance happeneth to them all.

Surprisingly good, for the Bible. I'll save Thackeray, another master on chance, for another blog.

ENGLISH AS SHE IS SPOKEN

I GREW UP IN middle-class, somewhat rural New Jersey. When I began to think about local accents—sixty years later—I figured I spoke "standard" or "radio voice" English. I had no trace of the New England "Paak ya caa"; certainly no broad mid-western accent, whatever exactly that might have been; and of course no Southern drawl, "ya'll," and so on. California? I don't know that they have an accent. You can tell I know next to nothing about our regional accents, but that is no hindrance to a few personal observations. Paterson, the second largest city in New Jersey and the city closest to where I grew up, had its own accent. The *a*'s in Paterson and Avenue (the latter almost invariably shortened to "Av") were pronounced like the *a* in past (American not British version), and with a distinct nasal ring. But I never used the Paterson *a* except as a joke. Besides, Paterson had nothing like the much-derided accents of Jersey City and Brooklyn.

However, a year or two ago, I was caught up in what must be a New Jerseyism of some kind by Meryl, my Significant Other. I'm not fond of this relatively old neologism, but Meryl is not my wife. And "de facto wife" sounds weird or even suspicious; so does "girlfriend" at our age; "lady friend" is better but still not exactly on target. What to call one's partner after 17 years of going together since the death of one's wife? Perhaps "partner"? In any case, my partner recently told me I was speaking like a New Jersey native because of one word: "won't." I was pronouncing it as if it were "wUn't," not "wOn't." No one had ever told this college grad, former priest, PhD, and professor (of English!) for forty years that all his life he had been messing up that word.

I was able to get even (sort of) with Meryl, who, though born and brought up in Brooklyn, specifically the largely Jewish Midwood section (Woody Allen was a high school classmate), speaks perfect English–like me, except, again like me, for one word: "hanger," as in coat hanger. She has a slightly hard *g*. When I jokingly try to correct her, she cannot help but repeat that prominent consonant– as in the *g* in anger.

Granted, we are not talking dees, dems and dos, but Meryl's "hanger" and my "won't" are curiosities if not outright lapses from that elusive standard English. I think of another instance. My dear mother spoke good English. The child of German immigrants of the 1890s, she had no foreign accent. (Although fluent in German, she never spoke the language: "We are always at war with them," she once sadly told me.) But one time, she slipped into a pronunciation betraying her upbringing in Jersey City, "terlet" for toilet, and my younger sister and I never let her forget it. We used to kid her all the time, claiming (falsely) that she said "erl" for oil, and by a kind of extension, "boil" for boy, "goil for girl," etc. On a different but still language-related note, we persuaded her that "crappy" was simply the equivalent of "bad." Once convinced, she said to a visiting church dignitary, "Crappy weather we're having, isn't it, Monsignor?" If there were a god, might he forgive us?

But by what right am I so high and mighty about "correct" English? As anyone who has studied the matter will tell you, language is usage; and no version of a language is better than another. Of course we have been so instructed and we all know that. I don't believe it.

WHAT'S YOUR NAME?

TO BEGIN, I'M technically only an "Honorary" alte kaker because I am not Jewish, although I don't see why a non-Jew can't be an "old shitter." At 88 and talkative I feel pretty close to the real thing. (And yes, various spellings exist for this colorful Yiddish moniker: alter kaker, alter kacker, alte cocker, altacocka, and others. But alte kaker sounds phonetically good to me.)

Actually, my real name is the problem. My advice to anyone thinking about it, for oneself or for one's children, is to be wary of using one's middle name. All my life this has been a problem. My parents intended to call me Jack, while of course acknowledging that Jack was—at least in those times—the nickname for John. And they planned on giving me a middle name after my father, Norman. But either my parents or the authorities at St Mary's Hospital, Orange, New Jersey, mixed things up, and my birth certificate—one that looks like a diploma and has footprints on the back—has "Norman John Hall." But I was always Jack to my family and my friends.

But come first grade, the nuns at St Aloysius School, Caldwell, New Jersey, would have none of that: "You are John." I of course agreed (there was no arguing with the nuns a Catholic school). And so to my teachers and on report cards I remained John Hall, at least until college. At that time, asked for a middle initial, I incorrectly gave N.

But more official documents, those, for example, for the Selective Service or a driver's license, had to have it correct, either Norman John or Norman J or N John. I opted for the last, and for at least 70 years I have been N John or N J (like in the state, I used to say). To this day, Social Security mail comes addressed to Norman J, J Norman, Norman John, and sometimes, my preferred N John Hall.

Two problems have persisted all these years: First, people ask, what does the N stand for? For some unknown reason, I don't tell them. (It happened as recently as when I was getting the Covid19 vaccine.) I do not at all dislike the name Norman, and I worshipped my father. I just don't want anyone using Norman for my first name, or even my middle name. Why give inquisitive people the satisfaction of knowing what the N stands for? (My smart aleck pal Jim Kincaid combined, for private consumption, "N John" into "Engine.") But nosy folks persist in asking: Is it Norbert? Nathaniel? Nathan? Some even try Norman. But I won't give in. "I never tell," I say. Or better, "It stands for 'Nice'." And sometimes, "It's just an initial, N, a mere affectation—it's meant to sound aristocratic, or Jesuitical."

The other problem is filling out forms that can't accommodate an initial initial, or, worse, the person on the phone taking down one's information:

>Your first Name?
>N, the initial N.
>Yes, but what your first name?
>That's it. N. I go by my middle name, John.
>OK, so John's you first name. What's your middle initial?
>N?

And so on, almost indefinitely.

One more thing. Many young people today simply won't believe it when I tell them Jack is the accepted and widely-used nickname for

John. "Huh?" they say. "It's like Johnny for John," I explain. "Yeah, everybody knows that, but *Jack*?" Sometimes I ask teenagers if they have heard of John F Kennedy: "Sort of," some answer. "Well," I say, "wasn't he also called Jack Kennedy?" "Maybe. If you say so."

It doesn't matter. But do avoid, if possible, "going by" a middle name. It's not worth the trouble.

IN THE BRONX

I ARRIVED FOR my first term at Bronx Community College in September 1970. Open Admissions arrived at the same time. Previously there had been vigorous demonstrations, especially at City College in Harlem, with the chant "Open it up or shut it down." The city fathers and CUNY administrators decided to open it up. Henceforth, all New York City high school graduates would be guaranteed a place in one of the 18 CUNY schools. Open Admissions did not mean that any such graduate could simply stroll into City College, or Hunter College, or Brooklyn College. Applicants had to list their college preferences but were assigned according to their academic scores. Naturally, everybody wanted admission to a four-year school, and many students wanted to stay in their own borough; and in the Bronx, most applicants put Lehman College at the top of their list but would end up at Bronx Community. The onrush of students was almost overwhelming. In those first few years the student population at BCC approached 14,000. Today it is around 8,000. The place, a proverbial beehive of activity, went bustling until 10 every night.

In any case, here I was, a fresh PhD from NYU, and if truth be told, a trifle disappointed. Like other graduates of a place like NYU, I would have preferred to be teaching at, if not a comparable institution, at least at a good four-year college or university. However, the job market in the humanities was already very tight in 1970 (unlike in the 1950s when, for example, my friend Gerhard Joseph, who had an MA from Minnesota, was wandering through the Modern Language Association convention hiring area, when he, without really asking, was recruited by Georgetown and hired to teach there). I had sent out about 75 letters seeking employment. My credentials looked good: high grades, various fellowships and NYU awards, excellent letters of recommendation, and a contract for a book with Oxford University Press. I got one nibble, from the University of New Hampshire, expressing interest in following up with me—an interest which was mysteriously withdrawn a few weeks later, the chairman writing that he suspected I was "a New York kind of person rather than a New Hampshire type." When late in the day there came the appointment to Bronx Community College, I was delighted. Because of Open Admissions the school was hiring so many professors that my appointment came as a form letter, on a blue-ink Asograph (the primitive forerunner of the Xerox), with blanks for the department, the appointee's name, rank, and salary to be filled in by the secretary of the hiring department.

When I came to teach that first semester, Bronx Community College was not situated in its current beautiful location, what had been the "uptown campus" of New York University (designed by Stanford White and considered by many to be his masterpiece). No, in those days the college consisted of some six or seven ramshackle buildings (including a converted bowling alley that housed the English department offices). Makeshift classrooms were scattered around Fordham Road and Jerome Avenue, the latter with its elevated 4 Train roaring on overhead, reminding you of where you were. Bronx Community College was securely embedded in its community, which was Hispanic and Black.

16

The students, then and now, are frequently unprepared for "higher education." Their high school scholastic records do not indicate that they are prime college material. On the other hand, I came to admire them for skills that I had never even had to think about. Chiefly, survival skills. My students, many older than the usual college age, dealt with poverty (many could not afford the textbooks until some specific financial aid arrived), the threat of homelessness, the need to work to support themselves or their children while squeezing in college courses, and troubles with the law (many had fathers, brothers, or husbands in prison). That graduation rates turned out to be appallingly low was no surprise. The dream of moving on after two years to a four-year "senior" CUNY college often went unfulfilled, as did the dream of at least a two-year degree. But for those who persevered, that degree could raise its possessor from, say, bank teller, to chief teller, even to "personal banker." I came to know of such cases. That degree meant an entry into the middle-class, at first the lower middle-class, but still, a move up the ladder. I came to "believe" in this kind of remedial education. It became clear to me that BCC was a special kind of place, offering an opportunity for the working class, the immigrant class, the poverty stricken, to rise despite fearful odds. Children of middle-class parents will get into college somewhere: if they don't get into Brown, it will be Bard, or Iona, or whatever. But for my students, BCC was their only chance of college. Of course, it's wrong-headed to think that not going to college is a disaster; there are plenty of decent careers that do not require a college education. But if in the South Bronx an underprepared person wanted to go to college, BCC was it.

To return to that first semester. The teaching load was about twice that of a four-year college professor. My first assignment included two remedial writing courses, one freshman composition course, and one "advanced" course, "Introduction to Drama." The overcrowding at the college showed itself in that one of my courses was taught in the open reading area of the library, a section cordoned off for me and 25 remedial writing students. (It was here that I was "observed" by two senior faculty members and managed to get through that potential hiccup on the way to tenure, five years and ten semesters on.) And the drama course was held in a room rented from a synagogue located all the way over on the Grand Concourse. I took these second-year students through a survey of high points, starting with *Oedipus the King* and finishing with *A Raisin in the Sun*. It happened that one student, although talented and on the student-body governing committee, had practically never attended class, did little of the work, and was clearly failing the course. He came to see me and pleaded that I pass him, on the grounds that if he failed, he would be kicked out of school, drafted, sent to Vietnam, and likely killed. I asked him "not to lay that on me," but urged him to do his best to catch up. My memory is fuzzy on the outcome, but I am nearly sure that this first-time professor, so deeply against the Vietnam War, gave him a C.

ON NOT LEARNING GREEK

THE RC CHURCH as recently as the 1950s had all its candidates for the priesthood, before they entered upon four years of theological pursuits, spend four years getting an undergraduate degree. In my case, the college BA was from Seton Hall; the first two years focused on Latin and Greek, the third and fourth on medieval philosophy. Of what possible use such learning—and granted it was very slight—could be for future parish priests was never apparent to me. Parish priests spend their days teaching religion, visiting the sick, overseeing Boy Scout and Girl Scout troops, running dances, accompanying basketball teams, "preparing" couples for marriage, and other such mundane work, employments fantastically remote from trying to translate the *Odyssey* or to understand Thomas Aquinas on the nature of angels. Of course, back then the Mass was said in Latin, but a year or two of high-school Latin would have provided enough familiarity with the language for that function.

Looking back, I see the smattering of Greek as the least preparative for parochial duties. Still, however meager and useless in a practical sense those Greek studies were, I recall them with affection. Father Joseph Shea taught us "Beginning Greek." We never got very far, but it was good stuff as he presented it. The earliest lessons included learning the Greek alphabet and how to read and pronounce the language. (My roommate, Bill Giblin, always insisted he never learned even the Greek alphabet.) Shea loved to read Greek aloud to his class, and I loved to hear him read it. The opening passage of St John's Gospel was a favorite of his. "Listen," he would say, "listen to the sounds and the rhythms." And even if all one caught was one word, *Logos*, the word for "word," as in "In the beginning was the Word and the Word was with God and the Word was God," it sounded lovely. (Joe Shea, the poor man, as we Seton Hall boarders who served his daily Mass knew, was scrupulous, at least about the words of transubstantiation, the words in the Mass that change bread and wine into the body and blood of Christ. Shea kept repeating, very loudly, very slowly, *Hoc est*, then starting again, not stuttering, but saying again and again, *Hoc, Hoc, Hoc est enim, Hoc est enim corpus* until he got through the words of transubstantiation— "This is my body." The words must be pronounced clearly, Catholic teaching held, or transubstantiation would not be effected. We lived partly in the actual everyday New Jersey world and partly in a world of sheer magic. Most priests and seminarians took a casual attitude towards this dual existence. But Joe Shea could not. In contrast, Father Jim Carey, the University's brash Athletic Director, would "knock off" a daily Mass, which customarily took half an hour, in ten minutes.)

But my favorite professor of Greek—or of any other subject at Seton Hall—was Father William "Josh" Halliwell, a tall, thin, gray-haired, serious man. He looked like a doom-foretelling Old Testament prophet. In private life, Halliwell was fanatically ascetic, and once told a few of us that for a priest to sink down comfortably into a soft easy chair was tantamount to a married man committing adultery. He also asked us to pray for his sister whom he thought lost because she married into the family of "that Seton Hall apostate," Will Durant. But Halliwell, in teaching us "advanced" Greek, betrayed none of his religious extremism, and with him we arrived, after half-a-year with Shea, at the first lines of the *Odyssey*. "Here we go!" I scribbled atop the textbook page:

> Ándra moi énnepe, Moúsa, polútropon ...
> Sing to me, oh Muse, of that resourceful man ...

Halliwell taught us Greek with a peculiar sense of futility that delighted me. I saw him as someone belonging to another world, that of the questioning and critical intellect. He struggled to interest us not only in the Greek language, but in ideas for their own sake. I recall some of his very words, which he would repeat endlessly, never seeming to weary of the fruitless effort. As might be expected in a professor of Greek, Halliwell was fascinated with etymologies. He kept urging us to buy Skeat's *Etymological Dictionary*. Each week he would inquire: "How many have purchased Skeat's *Etymological Dictionary*?" Never once did a hand go up. He would shake his head, "Too much stadium and not enough *studium*." He was continually asking us what we thought of Homer's calling the dawn *rododáktulos*, rosy-fingered. And were we not thrilled with the Greek word *spharagéunto*, describing the Cyclops's eye as "crackling" when Ulysses put the burning pole into it? And did we not love the sentiments Plato has Socrates voice when he says that he was indeed wiser than his critics because whereas they thought they knew something, when in fact they knew nothing, he knew he knew nothing, and hence was wiser than they were? "What do you think of that, Mr. Jones?" he would ask Giblin. "My name isn't Jones, Father." "Ah, yes it is, Mr. Jones, yes it is." He put strange questions to us such as "What's the meaning of meaning?" and "Why does the pencil end here?" He seldom got answers, but he must have realized he was moving some of us along.

Halliwell thought just about all learning could be boiled down to Greek language and literature. On the first day of a new term a lay person mistakenly sat down in our classroom. Half-way through the opening lecture he raised his hand and asked if this were American History II. Halliwell told him yes and went on speaking.

So here I am, nearly seventy years later, thinking of those sessions with Halliwell in the ancient Bailey Hall classrooms there on that campus in South Orange. As for my Greek today, I am lucky if I can recall more than half a dozen letters of the Greek alphabet. With the help of that old undergraduate textbook, which still sits on my shelves, and through the mechanism of this "resourceful" MS-Word program, I could have presented that first line of the *Odyssey*, "Sing to me, oh Muse, of that resourceful man…" in Greek letters. But doing so would have been not merely pedantic but downright dishonest, implying that I knew some Homeric Greek. No, I can remember only that handful of words, and these I must set down transliterated into Roman letters. Indeed, the only Greek connection I can claim nowadays is to have recently read with delight the *Odyssey* as translated by Robert Fagles. This masterful translation stands out among the scores that have come down to us: T E Lawrence (Lawrence of Arabia), for instance, translated the *Odyssey*, drawing from Max Beerbohm the comment, "I would rather not have been that translator than have driven the Turks out of Arabia." On a positive note, one thinks of Keats' poem saying how enthralled he was in reading Chapman's Homer, feeling like Cortez (an error for Balboa), startled in "wild surmise" at first seeing the Pacific Ocean. But for us, one could do no better than be a reader of Fagles' Homer. My poor memory retains little of the details of Homer's epic, except for the famous Cyclops adventure, where Odysseus blinds the drunken giant. Here's Fagles:

> So we seized our stake with its fiery tip
> and bored it round and round in the giant's eye
> till blood came boiling up around that smoking shaft
> and the hot blast singed his brow and eyelid round the core
> and the broiling eyeball burst—it's crackling (*spharagéunto!*)
> roots blazed and hissed—
> as a blacksmith plunges a glowing ax or adze
> in an ice-cold bath and the metal screeches steam

      and its temper hardens—that's the iron's strength—
      so the eye of the Cyclops sizzled round that stake!

This excerpt, from the grisliest passage in the 24 books of the *Odyssey*, serves as a sample of Homer's customary energy and velocity, while also including a typical long simile. This translation suffices for me in 2021, even as it brings warm memories of Seton Hall and my brief but vain attempt at the Greek original.

SYDNEY SMITH'S HOME REMEDY

SYDNEY SMITH? Who he? Only Victorianists or early-British 19th-century students will recognize the name, and most of them will probably not remember much. Except, perhaps, that Smith was a liberal Church of England clergyman, eminent as a preacher and writer, who rose to become Dean of St Paul's in London—a very exalted position in the C of E—and that he campaigned effectively for Catholic Emancipation (passed in 1829, repealing various anti-Catholic Penal Laws in Ireland and giving Roman Catholics the right to sit in Parliament). He was a forceful voice for the education of women, the abolition of slavery, the reform of Parliament, and other advanced views. But any description of him includes his renown as a wit. Unfortunately, I didn't have to hand any instances of his wit, my copy of a biography of him having been sold off two years ago as part of an effort to reduce the clutter of books in my apartment. (Experience seems to teach that whenever you get rid of a book, you eventually regret having done so.) But, this being the information age, I found on a Google search some admired words of his. Naturally, they lack some of the "snap" they delivered when spoken centuries ago:

> Of Scotland, as "that knuckle-end of England, that land of Calvin, oatcakes, and Sulphur."

Of his Scottish co-founder of the influential *Edinburgh Review*, "No one minds what Francis Jeffrey says... It was not more than a week ago that I heard him speak disrespectfully of the Equator."

Of there being "no furniture so charming as books."

Of a Yorkshire squire's wife, "She looked as if she had walked straight out of the ark."

Of his profession, "There are three sexes—men, women, and clergymen."

Of some noteworthy people: "Daniel Webster struck me much like a steam-engine in trousers," and "[Thomas Babington] Macaulay is like a book in breeches—he has occasional flashes of silence, that make his conversation perfectly delightful."

Perhaps most famously Smith wrote, "When I hear any man talk of an unalterable law, the only effect it produces upon me is to convince me that he is an unalterable fool."

All this by way of introduction. In 1820 Smith wrote to a lady friend suggesting twenty ways to help assuage "low spirits," or what we call depression. I had hoped to offer them here. They were printed in Alan Bell's biography, that book I let get away, and my photocopy of the relevant page has disappeared. But, having read the list so often, I have more than half of it by heart:

> See all you can of people you respect and who respect you.
> Don't expect too much of human life—a sorry business at the best.
> Take short views—nothing beyond tea or dinner.
> Read amusing books.

Take cool "shower baths."
Be as busy as you can.
Watch the effects of tea and coffee.
Don't make a secret of your low spirits because they are worse if concealed.
Be as much as you can in the open air.
Do not be too severe on yourself but do yourself justice.
Keep blazing fires.

And there was something about drinking a moderate amount of wine, "as much as you dare."

Smith's list is very "English": a "pull-yourself-up-by-your-bootstraps" attitude, rather than seeking professional assistance. And it's 200 years old. Any help?

A PAINFUL CASE

THAT SAME FIRST YEAR at Bronx Community College, I had a brilliant, but unpredictable student. He was a young, large Black man with an easy laugh and a great vocabulary. He struck me as an obvious candidate for a course listed in the catalog but seldom offered. "Individual Study" had to be initiated by the professor when he or she could identify a student as especially suited for a particular English topic, which in turn had to be approved by the department. The course called for a single, well-researched paper. I'll call my student Henry. Henry had shown me some "experimental" poetry of his, and I recommended that he take one poem by the sometimes-difficult Dylan Thomas, research as many critics as he could find on that poem, and then offer his own thoughts. Henry liked the idea, and he came to my office every once in a while to show me progress. I got somewhat close to him. We exchanged phone numbers, and I told him he could call at any time if he needed help on the project. The paper he produced was very good indeed, and I would never receive anything like it in my next forty years at BCC. On retiring in 2010, while cleaning out my desk I came upon a copy of Henry's paper. My office mate, Julia Rodas, was in the room at the time, and I asked her to listen to the final paragraph. She could not believe her ears. I think I saved the paper, but I am not sure. It may be somewhere here in my unorganized and crazily messy home office.

But the story has a dark side. As I got to know Henry he would sometimes, out of the blue, say seemingly incoherent things, or at least things disconnected from the subject at hand. Some of these disturbing moments came over the phone, and he once told me his mother wanted to say hello to his professor. Of course I was happy to make small talk with her, but I sensed she was uneasy about him. Later she called me back in an evident plea for help: I was his friend at the college, and her son was acting strange, having psychological problems. I felt at a loss to do anything other than suggest professional help. At the same time, along with my concern, there was a fear, coupled with a reluctance to get involved. I didn't know what I—certainly not someone equipped to intervene in such a case—could have done. I felt helpless.

One afternoon twenty years later, I was about to enter the Citibank on LaGuardia Place, just south of the NYU campus. Outside was a large Black man with a begging cup. Henry. For a split second we were face to face, and then he immediately looked away and started to leave. *So did I*. I felt terrible. I still do.

FIRE

OUR NATIONAL NIGHTMARE—or a large part of it—having ended a few weeks ago on January 20, I went up as usual to my partner Meryl's apartment for a long weekend. It was so cold and windy that I expected we would order in for food. But she, in a "celebratory" mood, insisted we venture out for dinner. I of course assented, and she thanked me for "accommodating" her, words that manifest a healthy vocabulary for someone who four years earlier had suffered a brain aneurysm that impaired her memory but not her wits. Still, it was very cold outside. In the midst of the Covid19 crisis, most of the outdoor dining sheds of the Upper East Side restaurants were empty, even on a Saturday night. Once settled into a plywood cubby at Antonucci's, open on one side and with an overhead electric heater, we were still freezing. This restaurant, located on East 81st Street, our favorite in that part of the city, did its best. One new wrinkle, as far as our experience went, was to supply us with large hot-water bottles, wrapped in cloth and intended to be placed on one's lap or between one's legs. These did help, considerably. Still, you kept your gloves on till you positively had to use a knife and fork on your *vitello tonnato*. Even the silverware was freezing—I was going to suggest that they heat their eating utensils until the last moment, but I refrained. We got through the meal with the help of some red wine, my favorite comestible in all the world, but which I avoid lately in favor of white wine because red seems to keep me awake at night.

We came home chilled all over. Meryl retreated to her favorite chair, and I made a fire. How wonderful to have a WBF—as the advertisements term a wood burning fireplace—and how easy to get the fire going. I remember my father in the early 1940s nursing newspaper, wood shavings, and kindling before putting on a log. Today, it's Duraflame. You can't miss. Just light any corner, put real wood atop it, and *voilà*, a beautiful fire. Of course I feel guilty. Lighting a fire, sending carbon into the atmosphere, while getting, so the experts tell us, only 10% of the benefit of the heat generated, seems almost criminal. Still, it's wonderful to have a fire in one's New York apartment. Were I wealthy I would turn down my nose at a 10-million-dollar co-op if it did not have a fireplace, a working one, a WBF. (My own apartment in the Village is in all respects wonderful except for one shortcoming: fireplaces begin of the fifth floor, and I live on the fourth.)

I can sit for hours looking at a fire. To me, it's better than television. And sitting there, or lying on the couch, or even on the floor, gazing at the flames, I frequently think of our ancestors. (The science here is wobbly, but these are a layman's musings.) OK, let's just go back, say, sixty or seventy thousand years, to think about the emergence of Homo Sapiens—us—as surviving at the expense of the Neanderthals. Although, I'm told that scientists see evidence of the tamed use of fire among hominids going back 400,000 years. Any way you look at it, for an unimaginable length of time, fire had been *the* thing. It foregrounded civilization by providing light, heat, protection, the development of tools and weapons, and the cooking of food. To consider for a moment just the light that fire delivered: for countless ages, when nightfall came, all was dark except for the fire. OK, candles eventually helped—since when? I have no idea. Back to the ancient Romans and Greeks, or Egyptians? It doesn't matter. Until the electric light bulb arrived a hundred and fifty years ago, all was dark when the sun went down. Black night prevailed. The period of human existence during which we have been able to stay up comfortably after dark, in our electrified night, is a tiny sliver of the long span of evolutionary years.

What were our ancestors like? The people the comics (the "funnies" in my time) refer to as cavemen? We know next to nothing about them except that they were our great great *ad infinitum* grandparents. We don't know what they liked or enjoyed—if they enjoyed anything at all—except that they craved, depended upon, and worshiped fire. Today, electrons and their doings make the world go round, everything from lights and radio to television and the internet. Before that it was fire. Small wonder some of us cherish fireplaces.

ASHES

TWO DAYS AGO, February 17, 2021, was Ash Wednesday, the beginning of Lent. That's a big day in the Catholic Church. I should know because I was a Catholic from birth until September 1, 1967, when I left the priesthood and became, as much as possible, a normal person. Those old days included many years of Catholic schooling, grades 1-3 and 9-12, followed by eight years of Catholic higher education (I resist the temptation to put those words in quotation marks) en route to ordination. You certainly never missed getting your ashes in those times. Then, as a priest, from 1959 through 1967, I *administered* the ashes to the faithful every Ash Wednesday. The day was more notable for me even then for its run up, the day before, the eat-up-before-fasting Fat Tuesday, Mardi Gras, a reminder of glorious old New Orleans jazz. I understand that fasting has all but disappeared from the Church today, and as far as I could tell, even in my time the only fasting observed was that of meatless Fridays and no food or drink before receiving Holy Communion. What a pain Fridays were in our family because my mother, although a good cook, could not manage fish—and, moreover, one had to travel ten miles from our semi-rural home to the town of Pompton Lakes (where Joe Louis trained) to find a fish market. Other fast days were ignored, even by faithful Catholics. In the seminary, we healthy male 20-26 year-olds were given a blanket dispensation from all fasting (always excepting meatless Fridays) on the grounds that we worked so hard at our studies and sports that we needed all our strength. Lay persons got no such dispensation; but from my experience, I can confirm that these Lenten fasting days were almost universally ignored, and that this noncompliance didn't bother people. Would that that had been true about all the Church's nonsense concerning sex and birth control, subjects which, I can attest from eight years of hearing confessions, did worry people terribly—one of the many great cruelties that the RC religion inflicted on its adherents, and, to some lesser extent, still does.

But, to return to Ash Wednesday. Parishioners flocked to church to receive their ashes. Something for nothing? From the Catholic Church? Every year witnessed this extraordinary mania for "getting your ashes" on the first Wednesday of Lent. As a parish priest, even after the latest evening distribution at the altar rail, when you had recited the formula *Memento, homo, quia pulvis es, et in pulverem reverteris*, "Remember, man, that thou art dust, and unto dust thou shalt return," for the thousandth time that day, you would find, as you were locking the church, people running up and pleading for ashes. Savvy priests kept an envelope containing ashes on our persons till late at night when folks would come to the rectory, all excuses, but hoping to be reminded that they were dust. These "sacred ashes" were the burned remains of palms from the previous year's Palm Sunday—Palm Sunday being another day when church attendance went through the roof. Another something for free.

Here we are in 2021, Covid19 times, and on Wednesday I heard on the radio something about the New York diocesan authorities telling people they could receive their ashes distantly, or some such nonsense. Then a spokesman for the Archbishop felt impelled to inform the faithful that "It is not a sin not to receive ashes today." In all my many years in the game, I never heard anyone, cleric or layman, as much as imply that it was a sin not to receive the ashes. Have things declined so far since I left? Have even more ignorance and superstition taken over? Some of us ex-priests quietly believe in a "brain drain," thinking that all the smart priests of our era left the priesthood in the 60s and 70s. I admit that there were a few exceptions, Dick Rento and Tom Coletta, Paul Manning and Ed Ciuba come to mind; but in the main, or so it seems to me, the intelligent priests I knew all left: Bob Call, Jerry Pindar, Jim O'Brien, Jack Corrigan, Jim Tierney, Tony Padavano, Tom Murtha, and countless others. They defected into the so-called "real world." Today, for me, whatever foolishness and medieval fantasies remain, Ash Wednesday still invokes the old night-before New Orleans jazz music.

> Let's drive down or fly down
> To New Orleans.
> That city has pretty
> Historic scenes.
> I'll take you, parade you
> Down Bourbon Street.
> There's a lot of hot spots,
> You'll see lots of big shots,
> Down on Bourbon Street.

PARADISE

A ROMANCE. Not your ordinary garden-variety romance, but one concerning a house, a property, a location. It all happened this way: in the spring of 1989, David Greetham, my late good friend and colleague from the Graduate Center, was engaged to a woman, whose name I cannot recall. I met her only once, but I remember that she was a close friend, maybe too close a friend, to the sister of the famous Kate Millett of the bestselling revolutionary feminist book, *Sexual Politics*. One weekend David arranged for my wife and me to come to see him and his fiancée at a country house they had purchased together in Great Barrington, in the Berkshires. David and his affianced would go up Friday night and Marianne and I were to join them on Saturday. But in the middle of the night, a distraught David Greetham telephoned me from New York saying that on the drive up to the country, he and his fiancée had quarreled and driven back to the city: they were not getting married; they had to sell the house; and he was driving to the Berkshires the next day to make sure she could not "steal" any of his belongings that he had already put there. I told him he sounded in bad shape and that I would accompany him up to the country the next day.

Once we were at his place, David—although he was for the time being saying goodbye to all that—patiently explained country houses to me: prices, mortgages, taxes, utility bills, along with the attractions in the lovely town of Great Barrington, including musical venues, restaurants, movie houses, three good hardware stores, and its nearness to charming towns like Stockbridge and Lenox, and, especially, proximity to the Tanglewood Music Center. (About a dozen years later, someone wrote a book on the ten most attractive small towns in the U.S., naming Great Barrington one of them; the local people, not wanting more outsiders overrunning the place, were not amused.) I fell in love with the rural landscape, the farms, the hills, the town, the idea of having a country house. New York City, much as Marianne and I loved it, had begun to rattle us, with its excitements, its delights, its demands, its noise.

And so, after about five hours at David's Great Barrington place, I called home and left a message for Marianne, which in its entirety said "We are getting a house here in the Berkshires." She, having long wished for something like this, was overjoyed. I had always argued, sensibly, that we could not afford it. But something had happened a few years earlier that made a country house feasible. Robert Taylor, the late and famous (in his world) Princeton book collector, had left me a valuable set of Trollope books, money from the sale of which could facilitate this purchase. The decision to sell that cherished collection (a complete set of Trollope first editions, each signed and dedicated by the author to his son Henry) came more easily than I had imagined: I was swapping Art for Life.

The next weekend, Marianne and I, having made an appointment with David's realtor, Nancy Dynan, drove up to Great Barrington. Having last week's *Berkshire Eagle* with us, we stopped at a phone booth on Route 23, just south of the town, and booked ourselves into a B&B on Main Street. Nancy Dynan then showed us half a dozen houses, all unsatisfactory. One was a split-level (with water in the basement) and very like millions of such houses in my native New Jersey. Another was a shack-like place literally in the woods, with tree branches pushing against the windows. Yet another was not too bad but lacked a fireplace. What's the use of having a house in the country if it doesn't have a fireplace? We were discouraged, even though we had been warned that people often look for a year before finding a country house they liked. Being somewhat hard to please, we had made a list of desirables: an old farmhouse—preferably white with black shutters—isolated, no neighboring houses in sight, with views of the Berkshire Hills and open farmland, and located near a river or stream. Lastly, though probably out of the question, a barn on the property. The next day at breakfast, the kind lady who ran the B&B told us that in the Berkshires, certainly in Great Barrington, people gossiped not about their neighbors but about houses. Our hostess then gave me a copy of the latest *Berkshire Eagle*, and I spotted an advertisement for a farmhouse, 2.11 acres on the Green River, isolated, complete with a "Wyeth-like barn," along with the caveat, "Needs some work." I immediately called Nancy Dynan, who said she had not seen the paper and that this house was evidently new to the market, but that she was friends with the listing broker. She told us to have a late lunch in a restaurant at the top of Railroad Street, and she would try to get the keys and meet us there at about four. She was late, and we were tempted to leave, but she appeared at last and took us to 106 Hurlburt Road, on the rural, farmland, western side of town. We drove in through high lilac bushes, and there was a rambling old farmhouse, white with black shutters, no other house in sight—just the hills and pastures with *cows*— and a smallish, gray Wyeth-like barn (unrestored, thank god). The Green River formed part of the northern boundary of the property. "We'll take it," I whispered to Marianne as we walked up to the house. We made an offer on the spot and arranged a down payment. Just like that. All in two days. The house of our dreams.

Back in New York, telephone calls shot back and forth between the realtor and me. He was confident things would go smoothly, although he had some difficulty being in contact with the owner, Leon Botstein, who was in Hungary for an international convention of university presidents. (Botstein was a whirlwind Renaissance Man: he had become president of Franconia College in New Hampshire at age 23 while a graduate student getting a PhD in music history at Harvard; he had then become president of Bard College, where he greatly expanded the school's reach; always involved with classical music, he would in time hold the positions—among many others and simultaneously with his presidency of Bard—of director and principal conductor of the American Symphony Orchestra and of the Jerusalem Symphony Orchestra.) In the early eighties, he had purchased 106 Hurlburt Road so as to have a second home near Simon's Rock Early College, which he had just acquired as a subsidiary to Bard.

Then, we suffered a fright when the realtor informed us that a second bidder had entered the picture, offering one or two thousand dollars more than we had done in committing to the asking price of $225,000. After yet another round of bidding, I "boldly" raised our offer to $230,000, and Botstein agreed. He had hesitated, so the agent told me, and briefly considered taking the house off the market and then returning to it at a higher price, but the realtor, anxious, I am sure, for the sale, recommended to Botstein that he take our price. He did. This college president had many irons in the fire, and selling a second home was a minor affair. He was probably glad to be quickly done with it.

Over the summer, a mortgage having been arranged, I frequently called Marianne's office at Hunter College and said only "We got the house." And on September 1, we closed; Botstein, whom I would liked to have met, didn't trouble to attend, but left details in his lawyer's hands. That very day, we began cleaning and painting. We worked exactly like "weekend warriors," as the locals called people who acquired second homes in the country. Eventually, we entertained all the time, and everyone seemed to fall in love with the place. Sometimes strangers would stop and ask if we would consider selling it. Not a chance. 106 Hurlburt road was a rural paradise, and getting it was one of the great moves in our lives. We reveled in every minute we could be up there. Did I mention the fireplace?

An inordinately personal story, this, and of little interest to others than ourselves. Yes, except that it again underscores, as I have said in previous entries, the importance—the nearly absolute importance—of luck: David's house, his inviting us there, finding that latest copy of the *Berkshire Eagle*, seeing that advertisement, Nancy Dynan being able to get the keys and show the property to us before others had a chance, Botstein's quick acceptance—all luck. "Count your lucky stars" used to be common parlance in my boyhood days.

OF COURSE

I WISH TO OFFER an apology for so frequently in these essays using the phrase "of course." Not to say that there are not plenty of instances calling for its legitimate use. But when an academic, or indeed some other presumably educated person, uses the phrase, he or she is often condescending: "Shakespeare of course used those words in *Lear*." Translation: "You probably don't know much Shakespeare, but I do …" Or, when someone says, "Of course there is no such things as intrinsically 'correct' English." Translation: "You, poor thing, probably think there is such an animal." Or, "We know of course that no biography can approach objectivity." Translation: "You naively must believe there is some way of getting at 'what really happened.'"

Having made my apology, I offer an instance of a peculiarly apt maneuver employing the words. When my late wife, Marianne, and I had a house in Great Barrington, Massachusetts, a man knocked at our door one cold wintry Sunday morning, and there stood someone I did not recognize. His manner indicated familiarity; he knew me. But I, with my mild case of prosopagnosia (face blindness, of course) could not place him although I had assuredly met him. His name was Russell Oberlin, a jolly, friendly man in his sixties. He taught vocal music at Hunter College, where Marianne knew him. In the 1950s and 1960s he was considered by many authorities the leading countertenor in the world and indisputably the foremost in the United States. He performed and recorded with Leonard Bernstein and Glenn Gould. I still have some of his records, most notably the Columbia/Odyssey Monteverdi Madrigals with the New York Pro Musica—so beautiful it can make you cry. While his speaking voice was natural for a man his age, his singing voice, as he explained to us, didn't change with the rest of him but remained that of a 12-year-old boy, or of a woman. He was a "natural," unlike most countertenors who must sing falsetto. However, at age 36 he abruptly stopped performing. When many believed his voice was as good as ever, he thought he was slipping, and just like that, he gave up singing and came to teach voice at Hunter. (Many years later, my partner Meryl and I consulted him on things to do in Venice since he lived there three months of every year. "I'll only give you one thing, the name of a restaurant." The place was called Antiche Carampane. It's impossible to find: one gets off the Number 1 Vaporetto at San Silvestro and starts in the general direction of the tiny Rio Terà de Le Carampane in the San Polo *Sestiere*, as seen on a street map; next, one gets lost—we've done it a number of times—and starts asking directions, and eventually arrives at the restaurant. Meryl and I agree it serves the best seafood we have ever eaten. A family run affair, they had a photograph of Russell and his partner pinned to the kitchen wall.)

That's some background on the man. I did not recognize who was standing in the doorway, and my face showed it. "I'm Russell Oberlin," he said. "Of course you are," I answered. Then we laughed, both of us knowing I did not recognize him and that my "Of course you are" was a cover-up. Then he told us a story of a friend of his, a famous actress—I cannot remember her name. But after one of her Broadway performances in the late 1950s, a woman was admitted to her dressing room. She stood in the doorway, glamorous and waiting to be acknowledged. Our actress did not recognize her. Then the celebrated transgender pioneer said, "I'm

Christine Jorgensen." "*Of course* you are," replied the actress, embracing her.

The phrase has its uses, of course.

A RELUCTANCE

THE WORD "WRITER," like "artist," or "poet," always seems to me exceedingly exalted. Whenever someone asks what I do, or, in these days, what I did, I say I was an English teacher, or, if feeling more brazen, I use "college English professor." I never call myself a writer. But I did as much if not more writing than teaching while a professor, and since retiring in 2011 have brought out four books, two novels with the Boston publisher David Godine, and two others with so limited a subject as to require self-publication. To me, "writers" are people like John Updike, Philip Roth, Margaret Atwood, or *New Yorker* regulars like Janet Malcolm, Louis Menand, Adam Gopnik. I am not even close to being in their ranks, although I have published, if one counts editions, a long shelf-full of books.

The bulk of my writing was done in conjunction with my time in academia. My long involvement with Anthony Trollope has provoked people to accuse me (only sometimes jokingly) of living in the nineteenth century, or more specifically, in Victorian England. But then, if one started in the 1960s to be interested in the Victorian novelists, Dickens, Thackeray, the Brontës, George Eliot, Hardy, and my chief concern, Trollope, these worthies were only some 100 years back. The Victorians did not seem terribly distant, even if they were our great grandparents. We seemed to be standing on their shoulders. And then, too, Hardy had survived well into the 20th century, dying only in 1928 (a year I used to remember by identifying it as the year after Babe Ruth hit that record 60 home runs). But with the Millennium, the Victorian era slipped back, so to say, another 100 years. Dickens and Thackeray are today what Fielding and Richardson had been to me in graduate school—very remote. But this is obvious, of course.

Graduate school addicted me to the Victorians (the golden age of the English novel), and I came to specialize in a single author—something already becoming obsolete even in my time—and thereafter spent a quarter of a century working on Anthony Trollope. Sometimes, when giving a talk to "lay people," say, the Trollope Society, I would begin by saying, "While you folks were busy at work making an honest living (or at that more difficult job, raising children), I had the good luck to be messing around in Trollope." If I have any reader here not overly familiar with Trollope, I shall identify him with a line from the eminent Victorian scholar, Gordon Ray, who said: "Trollope was a great, truthful, varied artist, who wrote better than he or his contemporaries realized, and who left behind him more novels of lasting value than any other writer in English."

Trollope has long been a favorite with both general readers and with writers, the latter group constituting a very special class of readers. Countless writers, from the Brownings and Tolstoy to Virginia Woolf and W H Auden, from Graham Greene and Gore Vidal to Anthony Burgess and P. D. James, have marveled at Trollope. Early on, George Eliot put it well when she wrote to Trollope congratulating him on his mastery in organizing "thoroughly natural everyday incidents," calling this skill "among the subtleties of art which can hardly be appreciated except by those who have striven after the same result with conscious failure." Noel Coward would put it simply, "Thank God for Trollope." The myriad of writers who admire Trollope should help to knock on the head the fatuous view that he is middlebrow pulp for people who don't read anything important. Furthermore, over the years he has accumulated *millions* of readers, as I once demonstrated, altogether to my own satisfaction, in an article in the *New York Times Book Review*, the crux of the argument being that any estimate of a writer's popularity should be based on publishers' records, the number of editions, copies sold, etc. And very few of Trollope's books have been produced for the lucrative classroom market—unlike those of Dickens or the Brontës. Trollope is never assigned in high schools, only occasionally in undergraduate courses, and with less frequency than one would expect in graduate literature departments. The noted critic R. P. Blackmur, who taught at Princeton, proposed every year that in freshman English courses students should read nothing but Trollope: "Then they will become wise, they will become devoted, they will be serious students." It didn't happen. Maybe this is just as well. Trollope is a mature person's author. His subtleties are of a kind that rise above the heads of most young people and, for that matter, above the heads of many critics as well.

Then, I got interested in Max Beerbohm and worked on him for twenty years, ten of them overlapping with my Trollope labors. Max appeals to a relatively select few. He himself claimed that only 1,500 readers in Britain and another 1,000 in America understood or appreciated him. Nonetheless, he enjoyed a career spanning more than six decades. He became famous in the 1890s while in his twenties (he was friends with Oscar Wilde, Aubrey Beardsley, G B Shaw), but produced his best work in the 20th century as he became universally acknowledged as the foremost British essayist (and caricaturist) of his time. So many hold this opinion that there is little need to cite them. I have already quoted, in my very first of these musings, Virginia Woolf, who called him the Prince of Essayists and said she could not imagine what it would be like to write as he did. The litany of writers who admire and wonder at Max Beerbohm includes Henry James, John Galsworthy, Joseph Conrad, Edith

Wharton, E M Forster, W H Auden, James Thurber, Truman Capote, Muriel Spark, Tom Stoppard, and many, many more. To quote just one, perhaps a surprising enthusiast, T S Eliot (of all people): "Max is the defense and illustration of the benefits to a writer of the discipline of the classics; the illustrator, rather than the apologist, of urbanity and the qualities of English prose style now falling into neglect."

It is indeed humbling, bewildering, that I, a modest student up from New Jersey and from the Roman Catholic priesthood, should have become the editor and propagator/advocate of two of the great writers in the language. Doing so amounted to a wonderful, un-dreamed of, un-earned honor. An additional bonus arose from my two subjects being so readable and entertaining. I was once introduced to the country's leading Browning scholar by a friend who identified me as working on Trollope and Beerbohm: "Oh," he said, "you don't like boring writers, do you?"

So, when pressed, I say was an English professor who worked on Trollope and Beerbohm. I won't call myself a writer. I save that for the likes of those I wrote about.

A MAN CALLED LIKE

EUGENE KASPER (Eugeniusz Kasperowicz) was a young man from Garfield whom I knew well through six years, 1953-59, at Darlington Seminary. In the fifth year, Gene was my "roommate." We were not situated as are traditional college roommates; rather, each seminarian had a separate room, including bed, desk, closet, and sink; and between his room and the adjacent room of his "mate" was located a toilet, traditionally called a "chateau." So Kasper and I were "chateaumates"—forbidden, incidentally, under pain of expulsion, to enter the chateaumate's room. Such was the fear of homosexuality, that unmentionable enormity.

But I did not call him Gene or Eugene, or Eugeniusz. We called each other, unceasingly, relentlessly, "Like." It was a sort of joke upon the almost pervasive use of the word throughout the society we knew, Northern New Jersey. I suspect that many people today think the ubiquitous use of "like" in speech is relatively recent—maybe thirty or forty years—but it's clearly much older. In any case, young people do not regard it as odd, or newish, they simply use the word and apparently give no thought to how like-filled their speech is. Walk down any street in New York and if you are within earshot of, say, two 16-year-old girls, or two 30-year-old men, you will hear something like this: "Like, I say to him, like, just who do you think you are, like, talking to me like that? Like, I'm flabbergasted." Is the word there serving as a kind of comma? Does it indicate a suppressed pause? Or is it just some verbal tic? But aren't tics unusual, rather than universal? I wonder whether a French or Italian student in Europe learning conversational English is instructed to insert "like" indiscriminately three or four times per sentence.

All right—and that's two words, no "alright" allowed here—enough on Kasper and I calling each other Like. What else? Alas, he has been dead some 20 years now, but I remember this smart and funny man fondly. I had for some time been interested in Polish American culture and, however slightly, in the Polish language. Back in 1958 he explained, for example, how his father, an immigrant from the old country, would behave when taking his little son Eugeniusz to buy a pair of shoes. The weary salesman kept bringing out boxes of shoes in various styles and sizes, and little Eugene would walk up and down the store, "trying them out," seeing how the felt, etc. Then after an hour or so his father would be satisfied, and the salesman would wrap up the chosen pair of shoes, tie the box with cord and send them to the cashier up front:

> Cashier: "That's $3.99."
> Kasper Senior: "I'll give you two dollars."
> Cashier: "What? The shoes are $3.99."
> Kasper Senior: "Maybe $2.50."
> Cashier: "We don't do that here! $3.99."

Whereupon Kasper Senior says, "Come, Eugeniusz, we make no bargain here." And they would leave the store.

Kasper also told me how in towns with large immigrant populations, Polish "national" parishes were run by old-world pastors and first- and second-generation Polish "ethnics." These parishes helped keep alive the language and traditions of the old country. (In polyglot Paterson, national parishes abounded: Italian, Hungarian, Lithuanian, Syrian, and so forth.) The larger parishes were Irish

American, and the bishops and high officials in the diocese were almost exclusively Irish. The "ethnics," especially the Poles, detested this Irish hegemony. Eugene certainly did. Darlington students always produced a comic show for St Patrick's Day, which meant a night off from compulsory study. Gene Kasper was the only seminarian among 300 who made it a point to remain studying in his room. A protest, availing to no one but himself, against Irish oppression.

According to Kasper, Polish national churches were especially known as being what we today call "cash cows" for their priests. Especially profitable was the custom, on a particular Polish feast day, of the parish priests going house to house and blessing with holy water the homes of parishioners. A newly-ordained Polish-American priest assigned to one of these churches told Kasper how he was instructed by the senior curate: "You go and you bless every house. Keep moving. It's good for $10,000. You keep your mouth shut." Oh Martin Luther, where are you now?

A few incidents from the seminary involving Gene "Like" Kasper especially stick in my memory. The authorities censored any books we ordered through a tiny bookstore (an empty seminarian's room, open fifteen minutes after supper five days a week). Kasper, who knew Russian, tried to order Khrushchev's famous 1956 speech denouncing Stalin. Kasper was called in:

> Director: "Is it true you're trying to order a book by Khrushchev? Is this Nikita Khrushchev, the Russian?"
> Kasper: "Of course it's that Khrushchev."
> Director: "Out of the question. He's a communist."

I also recall also how in our early years at Darlington, we had had to take at least a half-year of the Hebrew language, and those who did well were obliged to take another half-year. Kasper, who mastered the course, sat next to a fellow Pole, John Paprocki, who never opened the book and would have failed the final exam but that he persuaded Kasper to give him the answers: "Come on, be a pal." The result, almost as bad as failing, was that Paprocki did so well that he had to take the second half of Hebrew.

Kasper also helped me. With patient coaching he taught me to say two Polish sentences that I could use to feign knowing the language when speaking to Poles:

> Rozmawiam po Polsku bardzo mało. "I speak only a little Polish."

and

> To dosyć po Polsku. "That's enough Polish."

Thirty years later, a visiting medical student from Poland told me I was the only American he had met who spoke Polish without an American accent.

LA BOHÈME

I JUST WATCHED *La Bohème* on Meryl's all-powerful TV. You just ask Alexa to play the opera and up comes Teatro Real Madrid from the 1990s. Even this recorded old Spanish broadcast moves me. The leads are singers I never heard of, Venezuelan tenor Achiles Machado and Albanian soprano Inva Mula. (For all I know, they may be famous.) That opera also magnetizes Meryl, who invariably comes to tears towards the end of the last act, whether she's at Lincoln Center or in her own living room.

A quick confession. I love almost all music, but especially old New Orleans jazz, the thirties American songbook—music and lyrics (… Should the teacher stand so near, my love? / Graduation's almost here, my love / Come on and teach me tonight …), German lieder (Schubert, Schumann, Brahms), flamenco, American folk songs, the Blues, and other genres. Recently, PBS taught me to appreciate Country Music. But when it comes to opera, I am an outsider. Just never really got around to it, never made the effort, and I do envy those who have a passion for opera and know so much about it. Oh, I have seen other Puccini operas and some Verdi operas, but for me it's chiefly Puccini's coruscating *La Bohème*. I am aware that some opera experts regard it as lightweight. I knew an eminent music critic, Mortimer Frank, who thought *Cosi Fan Tutte* the apex of Western art (he was otherwise very sound), but, because he has died, I cannot ask his opinion of *La Bohème*, though I suspect that he, as a Mozart expert, would dismiss it as "merely" popular entertainment. Well, as for writing for the populace, for entertaining the many, I'll instance just Dickens—or, for that matter, Shakespeare. (I remember a professor in college saying that Shakespeare had one eye on the stars and the other on the box office.) Moreover, the notion of zeroing in on one spectacular work of a composer or writer is simply the way I am. Perhaps there is a parallel here with the academic working on a single author, say—just an example—Trollope. To take another case, Thackeray: for me there is only *one* novel, *Vanity Fair*, and I cannot be troubled into looking back at his other novels. Opera for us being *La Bohème*, Meryl and I in recent years have seen at least four performances of it at the Met (the Franco Zeffirelli production which some years ago the Met management considered scrapping, only to be overwhelmed by the outcry among opera lovers); we saw another production, at La Fenice in Venice, thank you, and one by a little-known New York opera company. Then, of course, there are the innumerable recordings, most famously the Luciano Pavarotti and Mirella Freni. I expect I have plenty of company in my craze for *La Bohème*. I don't know about the experts. I am acquainted with one authority who shares my enthusiasm. Dennis Koster, who tried to teach me flamenco guitar a few years ago, is surely someone worth listening to. A teenage flamenco guitar prodigy, he studied with the famous Mario Escudero and also learned much from his friend Sabicas—the greatest flamenco guitarist of all time. Dennis teaches flamenco during the day, and, before COVID-19, went out literally every night of the week to some classical music event (anything other than flamenco), having season subscriptions to the Metropolitan Opera, Philharmonic Hall, Carnegie Hall, etc. Now, Dennis, who knows opera inside-out, names *La Bohème* as his favorite. So there's at least one expert. And of course Toscanini.

The interesting question is the same as that for all tragedy. How is it so enjoyable? How do audiences come away from *Othello* or *La Bohème* exhilarated by the awful denouement? We know the usual answers, from Aristotle's catharsis of pity and fear to the curiosity and disguised delight most people take in looking at a car accident. But I should expect—hardly an original opinion—that, at bottom, we love the *words* of Shakespeare, the *music* of Puccini. Still, it always comes as a surprise, how we love these presentations of sadness and death, the good old *lacrimae rerum*, those tears of things. It's part of what art does, I suppose.

WAITING ON LINE

I AM NO GOOD at it. It must be part of a general impatience I suffer from, even though I don't see that I am much more impatient than the next guy. I am, for example, fairly good at waiting in doctor's anterooms, or at holding the phone when trying to get through to Verizon, when they are "experiencing a higher than usual call-volume and wait-time." But my impatience while standing in a line is palpable. I just can't bring myself to do so, and, rather than wait, I would rather not see the movie or get the special cupcakes at the Magnolia Bakery in the West Village.

This kind of impatience means that I would not make a good Englishman, in spite of my being such an unrepentant Anglophile. The English are famous for waiting quietly, *patiently*, in what they call queues, for busses, theater tickets, etc. And I personally have seen Londoners waiting in their queues in so civilized a manner, with an almost preternatural calm—no pushing, no jumping the line, as we say here. This in turn reminds me that I sometimes feel guilty about knowing my way somewhat about that foreign capital while never having been in most US *states*. Capitals? The capital of South Dakota? I don't know. I don't know because instead of seeing my own country, I have been to England, chiefly London and Oxford, at least 30 times, usually "under color of research."

But referring to London travels is a digression. I just cannot tamp down my frustration with standing in a line. Nothing helps, deep breaths, trying to think of pleasant things, fiddling with my cell phone. This particular intolerance must be a defect in my nature, and I had best to acknowledge it and live with it. But one incident comes to mind where I was patient while waiting in line. Granted, it was a relatively short and quick moving line for tickets at the Tanglewood Music Festival—a Saturday morning rehearsal. Waiting there in moderate calm with my wife and two guests one August years ago, I was struck by how the senior discount and Saturday morning hour attracted so many elderly music lovers. This thought prompted me to wonder aloud to my companions if there were any venues where the elderly, instead of getting a sizeable discount, as was the case here, instead had to pay *more* than ordinary citizens. A fellow in front of us turned around and said, "Yes, there are such places. They are called nursing homes."

A TONTINE

DO YOU KNOW what a tontine is? I do because many years ago while editing Trollope's letters, I found him asking a correspondent that very question. And wonderful to say, in due course I became part of a tontine. It is an agreement, legal or informal, where several contributing persons acting together put something of value, almost invariably money, into a trust with the stipulation that the last surviving person shall inherit all the money. As it happens, five of us Graduate Center professors used to go, during January winter breaks, up to my place at Great Barrington and have a kind of retreat, which we termed a "Lark," and at one such occasion we entered into a tontine.

Here's a brief *dramatis personae* of the Larkers:

David Gordon, Yale PhD, with an undergraduate degree from the other place (where he was on the tennis team). Blessed with a brilliant and clear mind, a photographic memory, and a cool temperament, he was probably the most sensible of us all. A good cook.

Speed Hill (I used to say of his name that we could readily believe in a man named Hill, and with some extra effort, in a man named Speed, but that we could not manage the combination). Harvard PhD. He specialized in textual studies and was the editor of Richard

Hooker (you can look up Hooker). An accomplished tennis player, he would not "adjust his game" to suit my beginner's "inadequacies"; he was the only faculty member willing to direct a dissertation on *A Tree Grows in Brooklyn*. A good cook.

Gerhard Joseph, Minnesota PhD. Everyone by now knows a good deal about our late colleague, his acute contrarianism, his alert intellect, his omnivorous interests, together with a stereotypical professorial forgetfulness and occasional befuddlement. The kindest, most generous, most sociable of men. A non-cook.

David Greetham, Oxford-educated Englishman. PhD from our own CUNY Graduate Center. A John-Cleese-like character, textual studies giant, but interested in everything in English literature and beyond, always up-to-date on literary theory, but deeply absorbed in computers, classical music of all kinds, theater, and *trees*. Another good cook.

People wondered what we, men without women, did for four days. Actually, we did little but talk, and maybe put in a bit of work on some article or book we were supposed to be writing. Or we read. (Gerhard, always restless, brought a deck of cards for poker in case the conversation lagged, but no one would play with him.) The talk centered on the usual academic absurdities, the more unimportant, the more impassioned. Of course we also rehearsed charming non-English-lit subjects, such as life expectancy, retirement options, life insurance, health coverage, living wills, physician-assisted suicide, etc. And, as I mentioned, we entered into a tontine, although in our case an ersatz tontine, like a gentleman's bet, in that there was no money, nothing in the tontine for the last survivor to inherit.

We did not talk about love affairs or matters in any way pertaining to sex. Except on one occasion, the year that David Greetham, having been divorced for some time from his (third?) wife, was looking for a mate. He had—ah, the folly of his business-like way of going about things—placed an ad in the personals of the *New York Review of Books*. His advertisement must have sounded attractive because he received some 75 responses. By his account, he had lunch with almost all of these women, before he (and one of them) would decide to follow up lunch with a date, and so on. (Years later I encountered one of these candidates, and if I am to believe her, they shook hands, sat down, and he began introducing himself by fishing out of his jacket pocket his *curriculum vitae*. I don't know whether she invented the story.) At the Lark, David, withholding the names, read to us some of these written responses to his ad. Many were quite entertaining. Now David, so sound in almost everything, selected, as all his friends agreed, precisely the one woman of the 75 who could make the rest of his life miserable. We did not like her. (Julius Goldstein, a painter from Hunter, said after meeting her, "*Who* was that woman?") A snooty, superior, pseudo-intellectual, she insulted us his friends, and treated our wives with disdain. We other four Larkers, dismayed that David might marry this woman, deputed Speed Hill, the colleague closest to David, to speak to him about our misgivings. Speed reported back that David had listened but remained "besotted" with her. David married her, had a child with her, and spent the remainder of his days in court, fighting for his life, as she and a pack of lawyers drove him almost out of his wits and into bankruptcy. Ain't it a life?

Otherwise, those Larks were wonderful times, the cold, crisp, snowy January weather, the fireplace ablaze, the kitchen busy, the wine flowing, the talk unceasing, the laughs coming easily. But, you might inquire, how about that make-believe tontine? Alas, of the five of us who experienced those happy four-day retreats, only two remain, the oldest, David Gordon, and the least robust, myself. The youngest and seemingly most healthy, Speed Hill, died first; then David Greetham, and, only recently, Gerhard Joseph. According to an old New Jersey proverb, life's a crapshoot.

A NASTY RANT

WALKING AROUND the Village today, on a late winter afternoon, I kept up a kind of informal count of the number of mask wearers. Except for those eating food, I would hazard that compliance is between 90 and 95% (even the cops, long holdouts, appear to be cooperating lately). It would seem that in regard to mask wearing during this pandemic, most New Yorkers, or at least Manhattanites in my neighborhood, are not science deniers or fools, or folks who think that anything coming from the authorities, especially federal authorities, is an incursion on their rights, or that mask-wearing (unlike clothes-wearing) is for sissies or part of a left-wing conspiracy.

What to do or think about mask refusers? As anyone who has tried to argue with these people knows, it's a fool's errand. The refusal to wear a mask derives from a mind-set impervious to rationality, no matter how buttressed that reasoning is by common sense, evidence, and scientific consensus. To argue in favor of masks with persons who are infected by naive innocence, or by misinformation, or by plain stupidity, is, to borrow from John Updike, like trying to explain the internal-combustion engine to a dog.

Evidence clearly shows that not wearing a face-covering where required is in fact more dangerous to other people than to the nonmaskers themselves. What to make of this sad and distressing phenomenon? It's truly a horrible business, because not wearing a mask is not harmless, like believing in angels or indulgences or a harem-like after-life, or, for that matter, believing in a loving creator. Such superstitions are mostly harmless, but refusing to wear a mask is not. These unmasked people are imperiling others; theirs is not a simple case of vanity or machismo, innocence or stupidity. No, such behavior is immoral, an offence against their fellows. But, as just about everyone knows, and as I have already insisted above, there is no reasoning against deeply felt delusions. You might just as well, to borrow this time from David Sedaris, try to explain the 1040 Tax Form to a squirrel.

But I find myself entertaining one thought that I have never seen set forth in print, perhaps because it is too harsh. Nonetheless, here goes: It's the idea that these mask-refusers may be of some help to the general society by themselves contracting Covid-19 (and eventually getting better, if their merciful god so wills) and then re-entering society with enough antibodies to assist that society in arriving at the hoped-for herd immunity. Terrible thing, to wish that some people will get the virus and thereby, in their roundabout, innocent, misinformed, stupid, dangerous-to-others manner, contribute toward victory over Covid. Excuse the pejoratives, but the situation cries out.

YOU CALL THIS FUN?

WHEN I WAS in graduate school, Professor Gordon Ray penciled a note on a paper of mine telling me that I had not yet mastered the parenthesis within a parenthesis, an aside within an aside. Fifty years on, I have still not mastered the problem. But at this point I am tempted to follow the example of Harold Ross. That astounding head of the *New Yorker*, who, after much back and forth about some editing problem and having decided it was insolvable, would wave it aside with "The hell with it."

So, in these reflections, when I break many of the "rules" of prose writing, especially that of unity, of sticking to the main point, I say the hell with it. Thus I won't be worried if while writing about, for instance, the ease of "looking things up" on the internet, I find this reminding me of baseball manager Casey Stengel, who, when asked by reporters how he thought his team would do next year, told them they could look it up; and this in turn reminds me of James Thurber's 1941 story called "You Could Look It Up" in which the manager of a mythical Columbus Ohio major league baseball team sends a midget up to bat in hopes of getting a walk (he hits a 3-0 pitch and makes an out to lose the game); and this reminds of Bill Veeck, owner of the old St Louis Browns, who, ten years after Thurber's story (Veeck always denied he was inspired by that story) sent a midget up to pinch-hit for a walk (Eddie Gaedel; who gets the walk);

and this yet again reminds me that when I was a kid the Browns were always in last place while the Yankees were always in first place, and how the Yankees cheer-leading radio announcer, Mel Allen, would say, "The Browns are coming to the Stadium next week for a *crucial* series," and so on and so on. As I just said, I'm not going to let the meandering or too lengthy a sentence, or the lack of "elegant variation" with regard to the word "remind," bother me.

All right, I find issues of grammar and style interesting. So I shall move this little essay—don't overuse the word "little," say most of the style manuals—from the unsolvable parenthesis within a parenthesis problem and dart to a (related) issue, namely discriminating among parentheses, dashes, and commas, as modifying dependent clauses, phrases, or single words, the kind of thing with which I used to beguile my freshman comp students at Bronx Community College. These punctuations imply, I would announce, three levels of importance. (I hope I did not just make this up.) Here's a "who clause" illustration:

> 1/ If the material in the clause is essential, use commas:
> Helen, who really loved Sam, married Joe.
> 2/ If the material is germane but not truly essential, use dashes:
> Helen—who remained fond of Sam—married Joe.
> 3/ If the material is truly parenthetical, non-essential, use parentheses:
> Helen (who once loved Sam) married Joe.

Am I "correct" in this? Not a good question. The above is style-related and therefore more a matter of choice than of right or wrong. On the other hand, some things require correctness, such as the use of commas in relative "who clauses." (And avoid "whom" unless you are positively sure of yourself: "The girl whom loves me" is illiterate;

70

but "The girl who I love" will pass.) Examples of the "who comma" problem:

"People who live in glass houses should not throw stones." The restrictive (no commas) "who clause" limits or restricts the meaning of people and is essential; it's only people who live in glass houses who should not throw stones. The rest of us can throw stones. But:

"Mary, who lives in a glass house, never throws stones." The descriptive (with commas) "who clause" is not essential; the sentence makes sense without it. Regardless of her housing, Mary doesn't throw stones.

May I presume here that my readers know this so well that my bringing it up risks (further) boring them? One never knows for sure, does one? And *that* sentence prompts me to close with a little—oops—completely unrelated trick I used to pass on to those eager BCC students. Try, I suggested, occasionally throwing the pronoun "one" into your writing or speech. It shows class. Then I would tell them of a (little) experiment I had tried with the checkout girl (as we used to say) at my A&P: I asked, "Where does one find the ketchup?" This amused her, and, ignoring me, she leaned across to her fellow checkout girl and said, "This guy wants to know where ONE finds the ketchup." Ha.

CUSTOMER SERVICE

WHILE WAITING FOR the elevator in the lobby of my building the other day, I heard something arresting. It was the voice of a woman screaming from one of the ground floor apartments. I could not tell which apartment, though clearly it came from the back of the building. (Although, one of the front apartments would have been a more likely source of distress because it houses a dentist's office. Years ago William Faulkner lived in that space. I occasionally pull aside a Greenwich Village street guide as he is showing his touring group either where Mark Twain lived or where the Statue of Liberty poet Emma Lazarus lived just a few yards away from my front door. I tell him about Faulkner having resided in my building here on West 10th Street. Why no plaque? He lived here only briefly, and the landlord doesn't like plaques or drawing attention to his building.)

But to return: I heard a woman, probably someone in her middle years, shrieking and saying "I have been on this phone for an hour, I am losing it, get me ANOTHER supervisor, not some stupid idiot. No, I cannot hold on or wait. You are driving me crazy." Then she would sob before she resumed screaming—as the same Faulkner would put it, "in impotent rage"—at her failure to get any help or satisfactory answer on the phone. Who has not suffered a similar fate these days?

It would do no good to tell her to be "philosophical" about it, to advise her to take the long view, namely that success or failure with this phone call will not matter in the slightest by next year, or probably even by next week. Most of us find it hard in such circumstances to take the long view, to be stoical. It's almost impossible to stay calm during one of these frustrating phone inquiries, those complaints we try to put through to our bank, credit card company, insurance company, or for that matter the phone company. But if she *were* to take the long view, what might that be? She could tell herself that she was not, for example, being evicted and thrown out onto the street; she could tell herself that she was not dying of some horrid disease—she was just being frustrated on the phone. But that kind of thinking does no good. This problem is happening to *her* and at *this* moment. That's how things work, isn't it? I am reminded of a review I read long ago of the Letters of the English poet Philip Larkin. One exchange went something like this: he was corresponding with a dear friend who was nearing death from cancer; Larkin was having trouble finding a Christmas present for a niece. He wrote to his friend that while he was quite willing to concede that the other's problem was more serious, still, "My problem is happening to me."

I myself am not in the least stoical about phone-call enormities. I get worked up even *before* I get to the actual person, the "representative." Are you not, like me, outraged by the recorded message "Your call will be answered in the order it was received"? Is that 21st century English grammar? Calm down, I say to myself, take the long view. But I cannot do so. It's just too awful.

WINE ANYONE?

IN VINO VERITAS is one of those half-baked proverbs that's half-correct, if that. Some people when in wine do tell their private thoughts; others under the influence tell more than their usual falsehoods. Either way, wine is special. For me, it ranks with the great discoveries of mankind, along with the wheel, moveable type, and mayonnaise. And it's such a complicated business: hundreds of varieties, many thousands of growers and brands—and each year its own vintage.

D'accord, the French think they have the best wines, language, baguettes (and all other foods), cafés, perfume, women's fashions, music halls, abstract thought, and virtually everything else. They are probably right about their wines. Years ago, I had a slight acquaintance with some of the great French wines, specifically red Bordeaux. That Burgundy produces even better wines can be argued, but I believe the best wines of each area are equal but different. If one goes by price, the Burgundies have it—Chambertin, La Romanée, La Tâche, Richebourg, etc. Burgundy's finest vineyards are fewer and smaller, and their output less; hence they are rarer and more expensive than the best Bordeaux.

But before pursuing a few thoughts about this giver of human bliss, red wines, a word and a modest proposal about whites. The foremost

Burgundy white wines, such as Puligny Montrachet and Meursault, are more famous and, again, more expensive than other whites. But I myself am not particularly fond of these pricey wines. My practice with white wine is to get an inexpensive, dry, light Italian wine, in my case Orvieto Classico (about $10)—you may do just as well with a Pinot Grigio or a Frascati—and drink it ice cold (contrary to the advice of the so-called experts). This suits my taste and my pocketbook.

My history in red wines began with drinking wine with dinner during vacations in my seminary days (which practice, if discovered by the authorities, would have led to expulsion). Next, as a priest, eating out, especially in the homes of my predominantly Italian-American parishioners, I found that wine with dinner was a matter of course, so to say. I of course continued this wine-with-meals tradition upon leaving the priesthood, moving to Greenwich Village, attending graduate school, marrying, and becoming a professor. Over the years I have had almost invariably at least two glasses of wine—or roughly half a bottle—just about every night of my life. I confess to having at times exceeded that measure, especially when dining out, and have on occasion overdone it. But for the most part I am a moderately moderate drinker.

In the early 1970s, having become gainfully employed, I embarked, along with an entirely new set of friends (Daniel Lowenthal, Herman Cummins, Sandy Wurmfeld, and Mortimer Frank, together with their wives) upon an informal exploration of the famous 1855 Classification of Bordeaux red wine. The details of this Classification and its history are complicated. Just glancing at it now is for me like trying to get up Algebra in an hour or so. But I do retain some simple facts: The classification listed in five categories or "growths" some 60 wines from the Medoc (Left Bank) region of Bordeaux. The ratings were based upon the prices commanded at the time and only indirectly on reputation. Even in 1855 the list was controversial, many arguing the superiority of, say, some fifth growth over a second (but never approaching the sacred firsts). On the whole, over the last 170 years, these wines have retained their prestige and their value. Our couples, singly or together, sampled these eminent wines at random. Once we jointly held a blind tasting of ten classified wines from the second through the fifth growths (you could pick up a bottle for $6.00), and Lynch-Bages, a fifth growth, won hands downs. Today that wine—or any classified growth, such as Lascombes, Duhart-Milon, Rauzan-Ségla—is very expensive, the result of supply and demand. Not just the French, but the rest of the world, especially the British, Americans, and Japanese, want these wines. A bottle of Lynch-Bages from a decent year now costs about $200, with others among these growths rising to $300 a bottle.

Okay. The *first* growths comprised four wines in 1855: Lafite Rothschild, Latour, Margaux, and Haut-Brion. In 1973 Mouton Rothschild was added to the list. (Because the Classification did not cover Right Bank districts, like Pomerol, it made no mention of Petrus, then and now the most famous and most expensive of all Bordeaux wines.) One time, we met at Mort Frank's house for a big splash, our only lavish indulgence, in which each couple was to bring a first growth. I was assigned to Latour (a favorite of Thomas Jefferson's), and had to inquire at three or four stores before locating a bottle. The price was $14. As it turned out, each couple preferred the wine they brought (this must tell us something, but what?). Naturally, all the wines had to be from the same year, and we chose 1967, a plentiful vintage but ranked only "good." Had we tried for an exceptional year, like 1961, the price would have more than tripled. Today a bottle of Latour comparable to my '67 is nearly $800. For a "great" year like 1982 the price is above $2,000. As for Petrus, one day, when the prices were still low, I gave Daniel Lowenthal for his birthday, a *half* bottle of that inestimable wine— of which he gave me a taste. Today an ordinary vintage Petrus is $2,500 a bottle, and, for 1982, $10,000.

In wine and other alcohols, as in so much else, we like what we like, or what we know or think we like. I recall an occasion up in the country when Mort Frank and Daniel Lowenthal were discussing the merits of various Scotches and agreeing on the superiority of Johnnie Walker Black Label over Johnnie Walker Red Label. I suggested a blind tasting, and each chose the first glass as containing the more expensive and "better" Black Label. Both had it wrong. But after flunking their test, they gave me a blind tasting of two red wines. I picked one as decidedly superior. But the rascals had put the same wine in both glasses. You talk about taste being subjective. That's one of the reasons I like to keep the bottle, with its label, on the table. Decanting wine is not for me. I know what I like, and I like to have the documentation, as it were, right there in front of me.

One more wine memory: for a wedding anniversary, my wife and I were celebrating by dining in a well-known French restaurant, and I got up the nerve to send back the wine. The waiter, as in any good restaurant, swept it away but asked me what I found wrong with it. At first nonplussed, I recovered and said, "It lacks character," a line I am proud of to this day. On the way out my self-congratulation was tempered when the waiter told me that he and the bartender had tasted the wine I sent back, and indeed it had "gone off."

Today my situation is different. Sadly, I find that red wine keeps me awake and makes me feel fatigued the next day. So I am reduced at home to that $10 Orvieto or in a restaurant to the house white, usually a Pinot Grigio or a Sauvignon Blanc. But as you can tell, I like to think about and romanticize those great Bordeaux red wines. Just hearing the names thrills me: Léoville, Vivens Durfort, Brane-Cantenac, Pichon Longueville, Giscours, Talbot. I sentimentalize the past, but why not? This in turns brings me around to another proverb: *Cena senza vino, giorno senza sole.* I think we can all manage that much Italian (if I have it right). And this bit of proverbial wisdom, unlike that I began with, stands up to reality. At least I've always found it so, Benedicamus Domino.

GERHARD JOSEPH

THE DEATH OF Gerhard Joseph (on January 23, 2021) has left a real emptiness in my life. Not to be able to read his email "geezerings"; not to be able to call him to ask how he was doing (invariably "fine," with never the slightest hint of the troubles of failing health in old age); not to be able to ask him questions (Tell me a little more about some aspect of deconstruction); not to be able to argue with him about a harmless point in Dickens, or whether memory was ever even slightly accurate; not to be able to know, continuously, that he was *there*, just across the George Washington Bridge, being his own singular self—all these losses add up to an immense void. I feel I must write something, and yet the hundreds of tributes (the most since Martin Luther King?) have said so many gracious things about him that I hardly know where to start or what I could possibly add.

But I'll try. Someone once said to a would-be remembrancer of another singular person, Harold Ross of the *New Yorker*, "If you can get him down on paper, no one will believe you." I can't presume to get Gerhard down on paper, but if I could, his close friends *would* believe me. People with a slighter acquaintance might indeed wonder if such a person really existed. He did, and the enormous outpouring of tributes to his brilliance, his wide-ranging knowledge, his capacious mind, his insatiable curiosity, his wit, his generosity, his kindness, along with his (more easily recorded) foibles, quirks, and eccentricities, have made the job of "getting him down on paper" so difficult that almost any additional effort must fall short or at best be repetitive. Nonetheless, I shall set down here some remembrances that may be peculiar to me.

Let's first see if I have any original or lesser-known "Gerhard Stories." All his friends know about his looking at his watch upside down and driving fast (for him, 35 mph meant speeding) to the San Jose Airport only to find that it did not open till 6 AM; his wearing his conference roommate George Levine's pants by mistake; his getting the date wrong for an MLA Convention in New Orleans and arriving a day early and wondering where everybody was. But how about the time the Graduate Center English Program deputed him to host a party at the MLA Convention in San Francisco? I know about this because I helped him bring jug-size bottles of scotch and bags of potato chips to the CUNY suite, only to find that no one came because he forgot to invite anyone. (When I recounted this episode to our colleague Morris Dickstein, who of course had missed the "party," not having been invited, he said simply, "That's why we love him.")

Here's another Gerhard story, one he told me over the phone. (It's funny how many of these stories revolve around cars. By way of background, for some years Gerhard drove a tiny, pea-green, stick-shift Toyota Tercel—a line the company discontinued. I often wondered if Gerhard got the last one. He had needed a new car, and being in a hurry to get such a mundane thing as buying a car out of the way, he probably took the first thing the dealer had in stock.) Well, one night, as Gerhard explained to me, he drives into New York, parks his car—lucky in parking, unlucky in love, he would joke—and late at night returns to the Tercel and finds he cannot get the car to go backwards. Luckily he could maneuver out of his parking spot by going straight ahead; he arrives home, leaves the car in the street—for how would he get out of the driveway if he drove into it?—and, first thing the next morning, he drives, straight forward of course, to the Toyota dealership, and explains that the car won't go backwards. The mechanic hops in and backs the car up. Gerhard had forgotten where reverse was. But, as he explained to me, he had not used reverse much, having put only 70,000 miles on the car. Is that story new to most Gerhard admirers? How about the time at Teaneck when he got a ticket for some harmless offence—maybe a U-turn or a parking ticket? Understanding that he had a right to appeal, he drove to the courthouse, had his case heard and denied, went outside to find he had another ticket for parking in front to the courthouse. You already knew that one? How about this: Gerhard and I ate out with a mutual friend and colleague, John Gaffney, and while those two were carrying on about arcane movies, I suggested that Gerhard give John a lift home as it was on the way. Gerhard of course obliged. But driving uptown he never looked at the road; instead he turned toward his passenger and talked non-stop about foreign films. John called me the next day to say he would never forgive me for arranging that scary ride. Enough of "Gerhard stories."

I first this met extraordinary man (and he was that; he was beyond, outside of, anyone ordinary) in the late 1970s when we were both hoping for an appointment, over and above our positions at our home colleges, to the English Program at the CUNY Graduate Center. In 1980, we each got the call to this PhD department, regularly rated one of the top 20 in the country, with the likes of Alfred Kazin, Irving Howe, and Allen Mandelbaum in its ranks. Gerhard and I, along with David Greetham, were the young Turks. Not that we tried to take over, we just wanted to fit in. We did our best, and hung in there for three decades—Gerhard for a little longer. I taught nothing except the Victorian Novel; Gerhard taught Victorian Poetry, Victorian Social History, different Victorian subjects filtered through psychoanalysis, poststructuralism, and god knows what else. He was an early disciple of Barthes, Lacan, Foucault, and Derrida, and was among the first in the department to embrace "literary theory"—which would in due course become the rage for a decade or so. Gerhard would in fact teach *anything*, as long as the subject seemed up-to-date. "I'm nothing if not trendy," he told me. We joked, he calling me a fossil, and I calling him a *doctor omnium*. (His lecturing was even more wide-ranging, reaching to *economics*, for god's sake, and—in the early days of the computer— on hypertext. "What do you know about hypertext?" I asked him. "Nothing," he replied, "but I'll have David Greetham explain it to me a few weeks beforehand, and I'll come up with something." His talk, he informed me, "went well.")

Regardless of what might be called our different orientations—I was the least trendy member of the faculty—we became fast friends. He lived in Teaneck, New Jersey, but would spend almost every night of the week in New York City, eating out with friends or attending some seminar or concert or show or special movie. And so for forty years, until the pandemic, he would come over once or twice a month, and we would dine at some Village restaurant near my apartment. Indeed, even during Covid-19 he drove over to meet me for curbside dinners and talk. His daughters (he has three wonderful daughters) and I would plead with him not to drive, to take a car service; but no, until the end, he insisted on driving into the City.

And what did we talk about while eating at the Sevilla or the French Roast? Well, the damndest things. From the first, he was so far gone on fashionable French philosophers that I can truthfully say that we discussed notions such as whether we were actually present in the restaurant, or whether the whole thing were taking place in our minds. You can imagine which of us took which side. Another explanation we gave was that our conversation centered on "Being, Non-Being, and women." (Gerhard was like Trollope's character Phineas Finn in that women all loved him.) As anyone who ever argued with him knows well, he was impossible: mild mannered, passive aggressive, endlessly allusive, always contrarian, ever ready to admit he would gladly take either side of a disagreement. I shouldn't say he could make the worse appear the better cause, but he certainly worked at doing so and enjoyed the effort. To take one relatively recent (2016) example: after Trump was elected, I lamented the fact that so many uninformed people had voted against their own interests. To this Gerhard would say, "That's your opinion. How do you know what is in these people's interests?" I would foolishly push on, quoting John Stuart Mill about the Conservative Party being the "stupid party," not in the sense that all Conservatives were stupid, but that the smart ones at the top needed a "constituency" of stupid people voting with them and against their own interests. "Oh, so you think Mill is correct, do you? Well, that's your opinion. How do you know Mill is any more right than anyone else?" "He's often right," I would say. "Yes, well, you think he is right" and on and on and on. Sometimes, while debating with him, I would in my mind step aside and see the two of us and say to myself: Don't you know he is deliberately getting you riled up? Don't you know he is putting you on? Why are you falling into the trap? Why do you do this to yourself? And yet such was his allure, his fundamental decency, that I would keep at it, no matter how maddening the experience. It's Gerhard, I would say to myself. After all, he was super-smart, marvelously well-read, blessed with an amazing memory (except for things practical), a good listener (to a point), and one who, always courteous, would never raise his voice or resort to unfair tactics—unless his just being himself could be considered unfair.

Naturally, we never got anywhere in our discussions in the sense of changing the other's mind, reaching any kind of compromise, or coming close to settling something. I frequently observed that if I asserted 2 and 2 are 4, he would counter with, "Well, that's your opinion." However, one time, long ago, he begrudgingly came to agree with me on something because it was in his interest that he did so. We were eating in that old Spanish restaurant, the Sevilla, in the West Village, and he regretted that, at 67, he was getting old. I asked him the date and year of his birth, and was able to prove to him, as I wrote down the numbers in ink onto the white tablecloth, that he was 66.

Here's something else about his conversation, either with me or with groups of us: He did not gossip about people. Academic departments and intimate conferences like the week-long Dickens Universe at Santa Cruz can be hotbeds of petty talk and ridicule aimed at anyone who engages in self-aggrandizement, bragging about some article or book of theirs, or worse still, simply boring his or her listeners. Never did Gerhard belittle or poke fun at anyone, no matter how much he or she deserved it.

I want to add that he wasn't at all "materialistic" (and oh, how he would have riffed on that word). He did not, for example, care about his clothes. An atrocious dresser, he just didn't give a damn about what he wore or whether his get-up was appropriate to the occasion. Once, he told a group of us how walking along a street, he saw an attractive navy-blue jacket in a store window; he glanced at it and continued past. Then he re-thought the matter, turned around, returned to the store and, actually bought the thing. It was a classy sports jacket, and he wore it whenever he had to dress up. On one occasion in the country my wife and I gave a large New Year's Eve party (having dinner, watching on TV the Times Square ball drop, dancing to Guy Lombardo's *Auld Lang Syne*, etc.), and we suggested, almost as a kind of joke, that the men come in black tie. The other male guests obliged; they either owned tuxes or rented or borrowed them. Gerhard wore that blazer and dark trousers and may even have put on a tie. A great effort, but he managed it.

Food. He was the least fussy person in regard to what he ate. Although he dined out nearly every day of his life during the years I knew him, he seemed to have regarded eating as a necessary distraction from talk and ideas. He enjoyed food, but indiscriminately. He liked the food of every restaurant he ever ate in; he liked a glass of wine but was never particular about it. After a funeral in the Village for a colleague, six of us went to a restaurant and were served a large carafe of white wine. It had turned slightly brown and was obviously "off." We all took a sip and agreed to send it back. "Tastes all right to me" was Gerhard's verdict. Another time, after some Graduate Center event, a few of us were somewhat at a loss as to where we should eat. In a moment of collective weakness, we agreed to follow Gerhard to an upstairs Brazilian restaurant on 46th street, a place that he "always found good." I had their Brazilian meat specialty which to this day I consider the worst meal I have ever had in a restaurant.

No, he did not care about clothes, or food, or Toyotas; he cared only for ideas (and idea-inspiring books, plays, concerts, operas, and movies)—and for people. He loved people. His talent for making friends I never saw equaled. To be with him in some large hotel lobby at the annual MLA Convention of English professors (10,000 strong!) was to find that he could not go ten feet without meeting someone he knew. But it was not just among fellow academics and their partners that his flair for making friends showed itself. Anyone could interest him and become a friend: people in the park near where he lived in Teaneck; people he met at the tennis court (he was a fanatic tennis player although hampered by an underhand serve, something, I am told, they don't even allow seven-year-old beginners to use). In recent years, he must have told me a dozen times how he enjoyed going to cardiac rehab four or five mornings a week because he liked the people there. The other patients and the therapists, yes, but also anyone working in the facility. It strikes me that Gerhard Joseph was the only person I knew who could have thrived in a nursing home: he would have become friends, not only with the nurses and doctors, but with fellow patients, attendants, the cleaning people, the security people.

Additionally, he generously helped his friends. I will mention one case. When our mutual close friend and colleague David Greetham was driven to financial crisis, his ex-wife with her lawyers taking every cent she could get from him, pushing him near to bankruptcy and causing him to consider early retirement so that he could get at his TIAA retirement money, Gerhard quietly arranged that some of David's friends each give $2,000 to assist him. (Years later, David invited each of us separately to dinner and returned the money.) Then, subsequently, when David was stricken with terrible physical ailments, including some particularly horrible variety of Parkinson's, Gerhard would travel up the long journey to Lenox, Massachusetts, where David had retired, to see him and if possible cheer up this man who for years was slowly dying. I don't recall anyone else doing so. I'll inject a personal note here, how when I was having family worries, he repeatedly told me. "Look, if you want me to come over, any time, even at 4 AM, just say so and I'll be glad to drive in." Quietly, almost imperceptibly, he went along performing, in Wordsworth's phrasing, the little, nameless, unremembered (almost unremembered) acts of kindness and of love, that best portion of a good man's life.

This last sounds a little grand, so I'll lower the volume and say only that in spite of the outpouring of tributes on the net, I fear that one facet of Gerhard's personality didn't receive enough stress: CHARM. He had charm, a quality hard to define, but, perhaps, like jazz or swing, something you know when you encounter it. I think he was in many respects the most charming person I've ever known—and I believe I have known a good number of charming people. But Gerhard had charm to an almost alarming degree. Even the few people who told me they did not particularly like him have admitted, in the next breath, as it were, that he possessed enormous charm. It worked with almost everyone, but especially with the ladies. I offer one very late example, from about three months ago, when we were eating curbside at Osteria 57, a restaurant across the street from my apartment. The evening began with his backing up his car next to the outdoor dining facilities and knocking over the owner's motorcycle (I tried in vain to convince Emmanuelle to sue him). Our talk had meandered into one of my hobby horses, William of Occam, nominalism, and a disbelief in essences. As the two of us were rattling on about whether such a thing as "horseness," or only individual horses, existed, I said to him, in an aside, "How many people in this outdoor restaurant—or anywhere in the City for that matter—do you think are talking about William of Occam and nominalism?" "Well," he said, "Let's find out." There were two positively gorgeous thirty-something women sitting at the next table, partly separated from us by the plexiglass anti-Covid barrier. Gerhard reaches around the divider, taps one of the women on the shoulder, and says, "My friend here wants to know if you happen to be talking about William of Occam and nominalism." Now if I had done this, I would have received a dismissive stare or a "Move off, creep." Instead, they showed interest, and the four of us chatted about nominalism for ten minutes.

Only in Gerhardland.

VACCINE RIDICULOUSNESS

NPR RECENTLY BROADCAST the news that the US bishops were warning their faithful that the Johnson & Johnson Covid-19 vaccine was developed from aborted fetus cells and should be avoided as "morally compromised," unless it were the only vaccine available. Apart from the sheer stupidity and willful disregard for realities, their report shows these mediocre minds slowly finding their way to compromise. They must feel compelled to do so because of how far the Church in this country has slipped from its triumphal days in the 1950s and 1960s, days which coincided with mine as a seminarian and priest. Since then, for example, attendance at Mass (a good barometer of adherence to the Church) must be down at least 80%. When I served in three parishes over a period of eight years, we had five or six Sunday Masses, so crowded that people had to stand in the vestibule or outside on the steps of the church. Nowadays parishes typically hold one Sunday Mass (two if you count the service the night before), with negligible numbers in the pews—mostly, I am told, elderly folks or mothers with reluctant kids just waiting to be old enough to stay away. Not only is Church attendance down, but also almost all the many hundreds of Catholic primary schools and high schools throughout the land are closed for lack of slave labor, that is, nuns. The ranks of new priests are down so drastically that the remaining priests often have two churches to maintain, and "missionary" priests from Africa are coming to the aid of American parishes. Moreover, the tenets of the Church are today widely ignored: hardly anyone pays the slightest attention to, say, the doctrine of hell, that hideous and immoral invention attributed to Jesus, the Prince of Peace; and even fewer give credence to that nifty brainchild "purgatory," so useful in the past (including in my time) for extracting money from the faithful via "Mass intentions"; and the Church itself has officially dropped Limbo, a chimerical place where unbaptized, innocent children were said to go if they had the good luck to die soon enough. As for the Church's thundering moral "prohibitions," they too have for the most part lost credibility. These days, almost no one gives a second thought to the "proscription" against birth control (or even divorce) although in my time the stance against "artificial" birth control was uncompromising and actually troubled people greatly: the use of a condom during marital relations, even when practiced to preserve the woman's life, was a mortal sin, potentially condemning the sinners to that fiery fairy-tale hell for eternity.

But today, the lightweights at the top of this sinking institution seem to be seeking a way out. No matter how sinful they view that vaccine's development because it used cells from an abortion performed in 1985, they big-mindedly grant that Catholics may nonetheless receive it, provided no other vaccine is available. Sixty years ago this kind of shilly-shallying concession would have been unheard of. All right, one might say, it's laughable, but what's the problem? Precisely this, that the announcement would be funny (the phrase "a morally compromised vaccine" is itself pretty hilarious) except that, given the fear of vaccinations, this kind of proclamation coming from the bishops—the spiritual shepherds of the still-believing—is dangerous. It harbors the potential for further frightening from vaccination some of those benighted souls who are on the fence about receiving their shots. Just at this moment the distrust of vaccines has increased as US authorities have called for a "pause" of J&J shots, not because they are "morally compromised" as per the Bishops, but because of six cases of blood clotting including one fatality, out of 7 million doses administered. Most experts seem to endorse the pause as necessary in the interest of transparency, but some apparently disagree. The *New York Times* quotes a virologist from Georgetown (a Catholic institution!) as repeating the already widely published fact that the chance of suffering a blood clot from the J&J vaccine is one in a million; she adds, however, that the chance of a blood clot from oral contraceptives is one in 3,000, and the chance of a blot clot from Covid-19 hospitalization is one in five. (On April 14, 2021, the day this was written, sources show US Covid cases at 96,682 per million citizens with a corresponding death rate of 1,738 per million. Who is for doing the math? Only a moron could miss the state of things.) Whatever one makes of this risk vs benefit puzzle, one can expect that the interruption of J&J vaccinations will be temporary, although the damage to public acceptance of vaccination may be longer lasting. The Catholic bishops' warning, with its begrudging concession, is relatively small potatoes; nonetheless it contributes to vaccine hesitancy and to the risk of infection and death. Granted the damage done is slight and is nothing like, say, the harm perpetrated in some in places in Africa where the Church-backed prohibition of condoms has for years greatly increased the number of AIDS cases and deaths. Still, such a communication is dreadful. A serious matter, this seemingly harmless, asinine, absurd caution from the Church's hierarchy.

I was about to say excuse the tirade. But these are the times that try men's souls.

LONG AGO

TODAY ON MY walk I stopped to sit in the small garden, open only a few hours a day, of the Episcopal Church of the Ascension here on Fifth Avenue and my own West 10th Street. The timing was special, because, it being early spring, the two large magnolia trees and the dogwood tree are in bloom. No church frontage in the five Boroughs—or anywhere else—looks more gloriously colorful or spring-like for a week or so. The church itself, one of the most attractive of its kind, a small brownstone Gothic Revival erected in 1840, could grace any picturesque English village or Oxford college. The interior, a remodeling by Stanford White in the 1880s, comes across as so High-Church that one would think it a Catholic church except for the lack of Stations of the Cross.

On my walks before Covid, when the church building was open every day from 5 to 7 pm, I would sometimes stop and sit in a pew at the back and collect my thoughts. Don't worry, folks, I am not in the slightest danger of slipping back into the superstition, fantasy, and wishful thinking that constitute religion; rather, I enjoy this beautiful, quiet place, one that floods me with memories each time I enter it.

I was married there (scarcely a hundred yards from where I now sit typing) on October 13, 1968. My mind reflects on the build-up to the wedding: It had been a year since I came to live in Greenwich Village with Marianne and to go to graduate school at NYU. I had in fact on the

Tuesday and Wednesday before the Sunday wedding completed the PhD qualifying "comps"—six two-hour written exams, with results not available for a month. A scary situation because it was department policy that only half the students would pass. Nonetheless, here I was, exhausted from that ordeal, and at (in those days) the unusually late age of 35, getting married. A few weeks earlier, after looking around for a non-Catholic church for the ceremony, I made arrangements with the Rector of Ascension, John McGill Krumm, who understood my situation and readily offered me the church along with permission for a Catholic priest, my friend Tom Coletta, to perform the ceremony. But Tom called me on Saturday, the day before the wedding, to say that Marianne and I would have to be legally married first because he was not licensed to perform marriages in New York State. I telephoned the Rector, who graciously told us to come in that evening with two witnesses. I then called my closest new friend from NYU, who told me, "Hang on," as he shouted to his wife, "Hey! It seems that Jack was a priest and they need two witnesses tonight—can we make it?" This "rehearsal" wedding went smoothly, as did the ceremony proper the following day. Marianne's family and relatives, who knew nothing of my background, thought it was a Catholic church and genuflected and crossed themselves.

The wedding was decidedly low-key. We had no money. Neither of our families could afford to help, nor did we expect them to do so. I was one year into my new life and going to school full time. We were living on Marianne's modest salary as secretary-assistant to a producer of classical Red Label records at RCA (Marianne would get me in to witness recording sessions by Arthur Rubinstein, regarded as one of the world's greatest piano players, and, I was pleased to learn, Jewish but agnostic). Money being so close, we invited only immediate family and a few friends, about 30 people. Photographer there was none. Flowers we did have, because a generous Greek American florist at nearby University Place listened to Marianne's plea that she could spend only a few dollars, and he supplied abundant bouquets and standing flowers. The food at the "reception," held afterwards in our tiny three-story walkup, consisted of cold cuts, a wedding cake, and wine. The apartment was so small that we had the "elders" come up first, with our few younger friends arriving later. The food ran out, but no one seemed to care.

For me those times seemed, *mutatis mutandis,* to resemble the early years of Hemingway's Paris. That's a stretch, of course, but Greenwich Village at that time was the closest thing anywhere on earth to Paris of the 1920s, and, given my egregious background, it was all the more exciting and thrilling. Hemingway closes his masterful memoir of those years:

> There is never any ending to Paris and the memory of each person who has lived in it differs from any other. We always returned to it no matter who we were or how it was changed or with what difficulties, or ease, it could be reached. Paris was always worth it and you received return for whatever you brought to it. But this is how Paris was in the early days when we were very poor and very happy.

So, begin by substituting the Village for Paris. As for my memory of the place, I don't know if it has been helped or hindered by our never having left the Village and thus never having to return to it. Surely the place changed with gentrification, the dying of restaurants, businesses, especially bookstores, and the exponential expansion of NYU. Still, much remains: the Square, the streets, the churches, the buildings; some bars, restaurants, jazz joints, movie houses, together with a touch of the old bohemian artistic spirit, and, again, the memories. The Village continues to supply you with "return" for your continued recognition of what it was, and is. And back in our early days in the Village we too were very poor and very happy. Hold it, I hear. Cut out the sentimental stuff and the ridiculous analogy. OK. I'll move to one other Ascension Church memory: Neighborhood tour guides invariably stop at the church (it's on the National Register of Historic Places) and have the group inspect the bronze plaque near the front doors that explains who built the church and who did the interior and when, etc. The inscription then adds that President John Tyler was married here in 1844. I am tempted, but have not yet mustered the courage, to tap the guide on the shoulder and announce, "I was also married here."

JUST THE BOOK FOR YOU

RECOMMENDING BOOKS is usually a bad idea. Of course if you know someone's tastes in authors thoroughly, you may be on fairly safe ground. It is not much of a gamble to tell a Trollope-lover that *The Fixed Period* is not as bad a novel as most Trollope readers think; it is fine to suggest the latest Guido Brunetti mystery, *Transient Desires*, to a Donna Leon fan, or to propose that the very first in that series of 30 books, *Death at La Fenice*, holds up nicely. But to recommend an unknown book or author to a friend is usually a fool's errand. For example, I was sure an old and dear friend of mine, a retired Oxford professor of English, with whom I have many tastes in common, would love the wonderful (to me) literary novel *The Elegance of the Hedgehog* by Muriel Barbery. He hated it. The only academic I could safely refer a book to was my late pal Gerhard Joseph because I knew he would never read it anyway. (Movies are nearly as problematic; people of similar artistic tastes often disagree drastically about movies.) You're about to say that tastes are of course subjective, and what else could you expect? Yes, but I'm speaking about a surprising *degree* of difference in reading tastes. The same Oxford professor loves old New Orleans jazz, and when I suggest a hard-to-find George Lewis clarinet solo to him, he predictably shares my enthusiasm. But books, especially novels, are different. Other friends, for instance regard with bewilderment my zealous plumping for Julian Barnes' *Flaubert's Parrot*.

It works the other way round, too, of course. When I asked a reliable friend for something light and funny and distracting during the Covid year, she recommended a book I found so unreadable that I cannot even recall its name. I judged another book recently recommended to me, *Native Tongue* by Carl Hiaasen, as disappointing, at best. That's not to say some of my recommenders have not been spot-on, as the English put it. My niece Lyn (the youngest of my "Three Graces") endorsed *Educated* by Tara Westhover, the autobiography of a young woman's escape from fundamentalist Mormon religion (where did Lyn get the idea I would like that?). Not only did she recommend it, she sent me a copy as if to ensure I would read the book. I did and remain grateful to her. (Learning that the book had been on the *New York Times* best seller list for a year and a half was slightly embarrassing. Talk about being up to date). Lyn also came through with a book so oddly titled I would never have given it a sniff but for her urging: *Lillian Boxfish Takes a Walk* by Kathleen Rooney. I thought it terrific and not just because it is about New York City.

Moreover, Mina Bernhard, friend, omnivorous reader, and—that touchstone of good taste—Trollope enthusiast, recommended a book that didn't at first sound appealing to me: *The Untouchable* by John Banville, a fictionalized memoir of the infamous Cambridge spy Anthony Blunt. To me it proved so fascinating a read and so gorgeously written that on finishing the book I immediately started to reread it, something I cannot remember ever having done. My aim was to enjoy again the original metaphors and similes displayed on almost every page. Years earlier, my colleague David Gordon had recommended, for much the same reasons—the style, the language, the figures of speech, the dark humor—Edward St Aubyn's five-volume Patrick Melrose novels. (I just fished down off the shelf the final volume, *At Last*, and sure enough the first pages of its high-wire writing again knocked me over.) These books so impressed me that I in turn recommended them to another of my nieces, Karen, the eldest of my Three Graces and another great reader. I just checked with her, and she replied that she had "loved" them except for the drug addiction scenes in the second volume—a caveat I share. Mention of my nieces reminds me that Susan, the middle member of the Graces and another intrepid reader, tells me that when she was *twelve* I recommended *Barchester Towers* to her and got her started on Trollope.

I am also grateful to my former PhD student, Julia Miele Rodas (who encouraged me to write these blogs in the first place), for bringing to my attention Julie Schumacher's *Dear Committee Members*, a book that quickly became one of my favorite campus novels.

But these positive results are the exceptions that prove, i.e. "test," the rule. (Excuse the pedantry.) For the most part, both recommending books and accepting recommendations are a waste of time. I'll close with an instance that exemplifies both the occasional exception and the usual futility. Years ago I suggested a book, *The Piano Shop on the Left Bank* by Thad Carhart, to a couple of talented pianists: one said that after reading it he could never pass the piano in his living room without seeing it in a more reverential light; the other said he could not get through the book. That's fine. One of two is a winning percentage in the mug's game that is book recommending.

SOME BLESSEDLY BRIEF WORDS ON SPIRITUALITY

I WAS ABOUT to begin, Oh, dear Jaysus, give me a break. And there I would have been using that interjection which many consider blasphemous, despite the crafty change in spelling. (Talk about a victimless crime). At any rate, this opening maneuver seems to me nicely akin to my much-loved figure of speech, *praeteritio*, or, as one friend is forever correcting me, saying it's called *occupatio*. But I don't need this "correction." It is incorrect as a correction. (Stop that!) A Web search tells us "occupatio" is also known as "occultatio," "paralipsis," "apophasis," and "praeteritio." The *praeter* I recognize from slaving through Cicero in college: the great orator begins a speech against Cataline by saying "I pass over [*praetermitto*] his crime of murdering his wife" or whatever it was he was mentioning by saying he would not mention it.

But I have scarcely gotten by my irreverent use of "Jaysus" and must be moving on to some heavy lifting, another instance of my violating the hope expressed in the very first of these blogs, namely that I would try to avoid "nonsense about things that matter" and stick to light-hearted subjects. Regardless, some thoughts on "spirituality":

A lot of religious charlatans and con artists talk about their inside track to spirituality. But many decent, sincere religious folk also go on in the same vein. This kind of talk, whether from actual frauds or the truly pious, annoys me no end, drives me crazy, and this in spite of my considering myself a moderately tolerant and restrained person. I grow more than impatient when, for example, Christian fundamentalists and other slack thinkers or simple religious people, folding morality into the vague term "spirituality," tell me or imply that I am less moral than they are because I have no reason to behave myself, lacking as I do, belief in a deity who promises me a (boring) heaven or threatens me with a (burning) hell. (People who study the subject say that atheists make up a minuscule slice of the prison population; some go so far as to say there are no atheists in prison, but that is probably an exaggeration.) It needs remarking that hope for eternal bliss and fear of eternal damnation amount to a second-rate motive for decent behavior. But let that pass. The same crooked or shallow or misguided people try even harder to corner the market on "spirituality" in a broader sense, a misty belief in big, vague, "ultimate" values, a state of mind responsive to "non-material" ideals, something they fraudulently or just stupidly contrast with secular humanism and science. It's sheer nonsense. I too believe in "things bigger than myself"—generosity, forgiveness, fairness, and so on. I don't want any persons, be they clever quacks or sincere believers, telling me that unless I acknowledge that a god or some Divine Force has implanted a "soul" or some interior spirit in me, I cannot appreciate these things or comport myself decently. (And, by the way, what could *sincerity* possibly have to do with it? A *sincere* belief that the sun goes around the Earth doesn't validate the error.)

Emphatically, I assert: I am as "spiritual" as the next guy, as are other people like me. I can do my best to aspire to the aforesaid generosity, forgiveness, and fairness, along with a hoped-for measure of charity, understanding, and justice; I am also "spiritual" enough to relish Shakespeare and Bach and Henry Moore; I can stand in awe at the cathedrals of Salisbury and Wells; I can revel in the language of Milton's *Paradise Lost* and in that of the King James Bible; I can respect and reverence some of the teachings attributed to Jesus, and delight in the smile on a child's face. The physicist Richard Feynman said that just because he knew something about the stars didn't mean he couldn't see the beauty in a starry night sky. Or, only slightly aslant my point, there is V.S. Naipaul's assertion, "I don't need some guru to tell me 'Sky big, me little.' I already know that."

All right, I got that out of my system. I'll calm down now.

THE GC

I LOOK BACK fondly on my thirty years in the English PhD Program at the CUNY Graduate Center. The students were some of them positively brilliant, others very smart, most all of them hard-working and devoted. (I remember beginning seminars by telling the students that I was at the head of the table only because I was older than they were.) By and large the students liked the place. I instance a poll, conducted early in this century, that inquired of graduate students nationwide as to their satisfaction with their departments. Our program came in FIRST. (I once asked President Horowitz why she did not mention this in public, and she said, "Because other departments did not do so well.") As for the faculty, we had some extraordinary minds, and all were reasonably smart, and most of us dedicated to helping students. One heard of stories—or recalled them from one's own experience—of professors at prestigious universities who were difficult, dismissive, or at best distant from their PhD candidates. Not so here. At the CUNY Graduate Center most of the faculty were, if anything, more enthusiastic about being there than the students. This sprang largely from our delight in teaching exceptionally bright and challenging students; at our home colleges, open-admission students were often—no fault of theirs—less than well-prepared for college work. Much as I enjoyed teaching my streetwise students at Bronx Community College, teaching at this graduate English Program was more like what one had envisioned back in graduate school. The Graduate Center was selective. In my time, the English Program typically received about 200 applications, accepted 75, of which about 45 ended up coming to us. We were different from other PhD programs in being so large and in admitting much older students, and also in having no full-time requirement. The truth was that we needed the students more than they needed us; they could have gone, had we not attracted them, to our chief local rivals, NYU or Rutgers. (Columbia was Ivy League, a step up, as most of us acknowledged, though the likes of Alfred Kazin and Irving Howe doubtless thought differently.)

The only drawback for us faculty was a relative lack of university-wide collegiality. Most of us professors—aside from a few full-time "central appointments"—were part-timers. We did not see much of our Program colleagues, much less of those in other programs: we came in from our scattered home colleges for one semester each year to teach one weekly two-hour course (14 sessions). The resultant lack of contact among faculty members was a built-in liability. If I remember correctly, John Henry Newman in his *Idea of a University* puts emphasis on the counterweight different faculties brought to each other. We didn't have that, but otherwise we were a wonderful institution, and we knew it.

Moreover, in spite of our limited teaching opportunities, we were on deck year-round for other responsibilities: office hours, committees, written and oral examinations, dissertation direction and defenses, and optional lectures and symposia. As for committee work of the administrative variety, much as I admired and appreciated persons willing to take this on, I avoided it as much as possible. My colleagues realized that I was not interested in serving on committees, and more importantly, was no good at it. One time I was assigned, no demurral allowed, to an ad hoc committee chaired by my close friend David Greetham. There were only five of us on the committee, and he peremptorily insisted that I take minutes. Reluctantly, I did. Years later, at my retirement party, David told the audience that my notes consisted of one sentence: "There was a lot of silly talk about curriculum and credits."

Serving on other committees, such as those for examinations, was a matter of course. For example, there were the oral examinations, where a committee of three would question a student for two hours about issues in her field. Of all of them, I remember most clearly that of a student who was recognized as not one of our best. Just before the examination began, her husband, a big husky fellow, appeared in the anteroom with a large bouquet of flowers. How could we flunk her? I remember one of the examiners asking her about *Vanity Fair*: "Oh, is that the one where the old man proposes to the young girl...?" We passed her.

For many years the written Comprehensive Exams included what the students called a "Trivial Pursuit" section. It consisted of 50 "objective" questions, calling for a simple identification ("The Hind and the Panther" / poem by Dryden; or *Sir Charles Grandison* / novel by Richardson). To pass, the student had to have 30—I think it was 30—identifications correct. Now as the answers were plain facts, you would have thought the examining committee would score this part of the exam pretty much unanimously. Yet seldom did the examiners come up with the same score. How come? Well, some professors were more lenient. I remember a conversation with a fellow grader about a relatively easy prompt, *Tender is the Night*, to which a student answered "A novel by Ernest Hemingway." I marked it wrong, while my convivial colleague, the Joyce scholar Eddie Epstein (students told me he used to *sing* parts of *Finnegans Wake* in his seminar), marked it correct. I asked him about this, and he said, "Well, yes, the student got the name wrong, but the author was an American writer of the same period, and the work was a novel. So the student got the answer 2/3rds correct. And I felt that was adequate." Fair enough, says I.

Funny, isn't it, how some snatches of time past remain in memory? I remember making a few "converts" to Trollope (having myself been introduced to that novelist only in graduate school). Moments after one of my seminars, I heard two students talking: "You don't like Lizzie Eustace? Oh, I love her." That is, they were speaking about Trollope's characters as if they were actual persons—the very thing he aimed for in his fiction.

Naturally, not all interactions with students were positive. One time I said to a class, that even as I felt inadequate about teaching James Baldwin, seeing that as a white man I had never experienced what it was to live as a Black man in this country, I confessed a similar inadequacy, for obvious reasons, in truly "getting" much feminist literature. One male student jumped up and angrily challenged me. He said that such a position if embraced would void his "entire career." I of course did not argue, but said I had overstepped and that my comparison was not apt. He probably never forgave me, not that it was important. I still think I was right, John Stuart Mill *et al* notwithstanding. (Our Program eventually became, in the opinion of many, the leading English graduate program for LGBTQ studies. I report this proud achievement as one who did not have any role in creating this eminence.)

A less serious mistake arose in another class from a discussion of the Victorian notion of the gentleman. After citing Newman's "Someone who keeps his eye on all his company," who won't let anybody be kept out of the discussion, I told the class about another Victorian definition of gentleman, and by extension, of gentlewoman: "Someone who knows how to play the accordion, but won't." Whereupon Susan Barile, a superb student, put up her hand and said, "Well, *I* play the accordion." I apologized, although she made a joke of it. Susan and her husband subsequently became my good friends and have remained so all these years. She has a book of Edith Wharton's letters coming out with Yale University Press, and you can imagine who suggested she offer the work first to Yale.

If that accordion joke was a light moment, a bad moment of interaction with a student occurred earlier, back in the 1990s, when Julia Miele, now Julia Miele Rodas, came into my office to introduce herself and to discuss some idea about Dickens or Trollope and religion. As the discussion progressed, I asked, "Do you believe in God?" No sooner had I uttered the words than I realized my gaffe. But before I could withdraw the question, she spoke up: "Professor, I don't think you should put that question to me." I immediately agreed, apologized, and so forth. (See the story in *Dubliners* where a boss says to his employee, "Tell me, do you think me an utter fool?" And the fellow replies, "I don't think, sir, that that's a fair question to put to me.") Julia and I have been friends and colleagues ever since; she even dedicated a book to me; moreover, it was she who (I will not say in a weak moment) convinced me to undertake this blogging business.

On another occasion, as we went around the seminar table with students offering initial reactions to *Great Expectations,* I was floored. One young woman, apparently a fierce political activist, found nothing but fault with the novel, condemning it as apolitical. "What's the point?" she asked. I usually am not at a loss for some kind of words. But at this I fell silent. The point of *Great Expectations?* I thought about asking what is the point of art. Instead, I said nothing and left it to the class; but they seemed unwilling to engage her. Maybe they knew her for a fanatic and figured there was no sense in discussing the matter. In any event, the seminar just moved on. I was later told that the woman dropped out of the program. No surprise there.

In another Victorian novel course, the students, all female but one, were eloquently celebrating *Wuthering Heights*, finding all sorts of wonderful things to say about that strange book. But one older student raised her hand and said that she was the mother of three teenage girls, and that while she thought it a good novel for them, she herself considered W*uthering Heights* comical and admitted to laughing out loud in places. I made no remark but looked admiringly at her. (A relevant comment that I did not share with students came from the late Professor Donald Stone: when the department replaced *Barchester Towers* with *Wuthering Heights* on a list of 50 novels students were expected to know for the Comprehensive Exams, Stone wrote to the chair and the entire faculty asking whether our students were not past adolescence and grownups by now.)

Another incident, a kind of extra-curricular moment that I am rather proud of, comes vividly back to me. Superstar Alfred Kazin gave a talk to a large audience, on a subject I cannot recall; and a graduate student, who was seated in the back row, put a question to the great man. Kazin replied that it would be a waste of time to address so stupid a question, and moved on to the next raised hand. Afterwards, I asked the Program Assistant, Lynn Kadison, who had been present at the lecture, to give me that student's name and phone number. The next day, I called him in Brooklyn, introduced myself, apologized for the Program, and told him to ignore what had happened, that Kazin was an intellectual street-brawler and that his words should be disregarded. I trust the student was cheered a bit by this call. I don't know, but I hope so.

These few high and low points still linger with me. A mixed lot, a farrago of memories. Whatever. I recall the Graduate Center English Program with affection, even with love.

THE ENORMITY OF IT ALL

SOME PEOPLE HAVE love affairs with words. That's the kind of slippery usage we all use even though we know that the analogy—in this case involving the old-fashioned romantic connection between two people—doesn't altogether hold up. But it will do. We love words and are sometimes insanely jealous of our notions about the meaning of this or that word or expression. For me, this possessiveness takes the form of an insistence on a single meaning for the word *enormity*: I want the word to mean "monstrous wickedness," not hugeness or enormousness. However, a controversy—an enormous controversy?—surrounds this word, and I would like briefly to explore it here. We can begin by dismissing its etymology (shared of course with *enormousness*) from the Latin prefix *e* ("out of") and *norma* ("rule" or "carpenter's square"). Although etymologies can be helpful and amusing, they often don't equate with meaning (*manufactured* etymologically means made by hand—the very opposite of what that word denotes).

Thus, to get down to cases: I wish to reserve the meaning of the word to great moral evil, like genocide, or other great misdeeds, like the bungled use of *I* and *me* in speech or writing ("Just between you and I"). This is of course heresy. Language is usage and usage changes. But I am suggesting that if we use *enormity* to mean largeness or great size we are weakening it, watering it down, lessening its descriptive force. So when a college president —I won't say which one—here at CUNY, writes of "the enormity of the task of revising the curriculum," I shudder (unless the task involved removing all humanities courses from the University). I was also shocked recently by seeing a writer for whom I have enormous admiration use the term to mean bigness. The multi-talented Adam Gopnik (admirable also for his devotion to Trollope and Max Beerbohm) did so, and in the New Yorker, no less, the magazine famous for its almost precious adherence to the old-fashioned prescriptive approach to words. So I figured I should take a look at what the experts have to say.

Good old *Strunk and White* puts it succinctly: *Enormity* means monstrous wickedness, not bigness.

Fowler's Modern English Usage, in the first two editions, 1926 and 1965, is firmly on the "my" side. That venerable guide says it is "inadvisable" to conflate *enormity* and *enormousness*, and suggests using "vastness" or "enormous extent" for the latter; it says that the phrase "the enormity of the impression produced by the building" renders its author open to a "suspicion of ignorance." Score one for monstrous wickedness.

In the Third Edition of *Fowler's*, completely reworked by R W Burchfield in 1996, the *enormity* entry is a dozen times longer than the earlier one. Burchfield relies on the OED to trace the separation of meanings between *enormity* and *enormousness* as growing steadily since the early 19th century, and he announces that "nowadays"—the 1990s—a distinct meaning for each word seems to be "pretty much" the standard. But he admits that *enormity* "seemingly cannot be kept within bounds and is encroaching on the territory set aside for *enormousness*"; he says that the real problem comes where "the notions of wickedness and hugeness coincide," as in "He did not register the enormity of his crime." Burchfield ends his lengthy discussion by reasserting that *enormity* should not be used for simple largeness— "the enormity of the pyramids." OK.

Next, I looked into the magisterial *Webster's Third New International Dictionary ... Unabridged*, 1966. *The Third* is famously applauded or condemned for avoiding almost all "usage labels" and simply listing the meanings of words rather than categorizing or labelling some words as colloquial, slang, vulgar, or profane. This policy was hugely controversial, with the "liberals" defending its "democratic" approach, and the word-conservative critics raging against the lack of guidance that readers expect from a dictionary. Moreover, these critics considered the relatively small handful of usage labels retained as inadequate and weak. In *Webster's Third*, for instance, the N-word is labeled "usually taken to be offensive." Usually!

As for *enormity*, *The Third* gives four meanings, none with usage labels: 1/ The quality or state of exceeding measure or of being immoderate. 2/ A grave offense against order, right, or decency. 3/ Abnormality (*obsolete*). 4/ Hugeness, immensity. Thus, the great authoritative American dictionary gives approval to the meaning that I find abhorrent. Doing so was in keeping with its stated object of simply describing the way words are used. So even sixty years ago my opinion seemed to have lost ground.

Then came the *American Heritage Dictionary*, 1969 and later editions. This had usage labels galore, determined by a panel of more than 100 distinguished writers, editors, and professors. The dictionary assigns *enormity* two meanings: 1/ The quality of passing all moral bounds; excessive wickedness; outrageousness. 2/ A monstrous offense or evil; an outrage. Then a usage label declares that 93 percent of the panel of experts voted the sense of "huge size" as unacceptable. But in the Fourth Edition, 2002, the number of usage panel experts disapproving of *enormity* referring to hugeness was down to 53 percent. Sadly, a sign of the times.

For an up-to-date assessment, I went to the web and was at first delighted to see that a simple Google definition gave only "monstrous evil." But, alas, a further look discovered the *Digital Merriam Webster* giving *enormity* a third meaning—hugeness—and a label endorsing "the enormity of the desert" and "the enormity of the task of teachers in slum schools." Such usage strikes me as substandard. But when the electronic dictionary embraces the word when it suggests "both great size and deviation from morality," as in "the enormity of existing stockpiles of atomic weapons," I must concede this as being close to my "monstrous evil" denotation.

It's a messy controversy, but one in which "hugeness" will apparently come to be an accepted meaning of *enormity*. Me, I'm sticking with "monstrous wickedness." There is so much of it both past and present that we need this special word to shine a bright light on it.

So no, we do not want "The enormity of the Statue of Liberty." But yes, "The enormity of Trump's presidency."

BLACK AND WHITE IN THE BRONX

FOR ALMOST FORTY years, I taught English at Bronx Community College, at first in a set of haphazard buildings around Fordham Road and Jerome Avenue, and starting in 1973, at a peaceful and lovely 55-acre enclave overlooking the Harlem River. The campus was pristine—one never saw litter anywhere, much less graffiti—a place universally respected. It was a haven as crime spiked in New York City, and students and faculty were conscious that the streets around the college could be dangerous, especially at night. For the first ten years, I didn't think very much about the potential dangers of my commute from Greenwich Village to the Bronx. During the day, I walked through the lively neighborhood from the subway to the campus and at night I would hail a so-called gypsy cab back to the subway. It was easy to get these illegal taxis: all you had to do was step off the curb and raise your hand, and a car would stop. It would not have a meter, of course; and you simply paid a reasonable fare. But one time a Latino driver, having stopped to let me off at the station, turned around and looked me in the eye and said, with emphasis, "Man, what are you doing here?" Shortly thereafter I bought an old Chevy Nova from a friend. As happy as I was to teach at the college, the driver had focused my attention on an undeniable aspect of my situation: as a white person working with and around people of color, there were bound to be some tensions. But, in fact, they were extremely rare.

Indeed, I can remember only two truly difficult moments. "Why are we not learning Swahili? Why are you teaching us English? Why isn't this a class in Swahili?" These angry questions were shouted at me by a young Black man, who was standing by his desk, in the center of a room with some 30 students. This was during my second year at Bronx Community College. I tried to stay calm: here I was, the only white person in the room and being harshly challenged. At first I said nothing, and then remarked that, for one thing, I did not know Swahili and that the course was called "Fundamentals of English Composition." He persisted haranguing, but I was relieved to hear murmurs from other students, ranging from "Sit down" to "Shut up." The moment passed. After class, either that night or the next, the student approached me and apologized, saying he had been out of order. Indeed, he often stopped by with some question or observation (he was a smart and eager student), and we actually became friends for the semester.

A much worse moment for me as a teacher, and one that was my fault, also came in those early years when I was still comparatively new and inexperienced. The students were discussing *Hamlet* and I was surprised when a woman, although not making any reference to race, complained that the play was no good, that its poetry (about which doubtless I had been rhapsodizing) was no good, that it was a waste of time, that it was all "meaningless." These words prompted the mistake that most stands out from all my many years of teaching. I replied to the effect that people who say things like that about Shakespeare are really saying something about themselves. She burst into tears and ran out of the room. After a moment's inaction, hoping for someone in the class to come to my rescue, I followed the student, caught up with her and apologized profusely. I cannot further recall the outcome.

Shakespeare was one thing, but how about Black writers? Was I qualified to teach them? In fact, during the time I taught Black literature, no one ever raised the slightest question of my suitability to do so. No student ever said to me, "What do you know about Black people?" But to be on the safe side, I took elaborate steps. Before discussing James Baldwin's short stories (as I did for many years), I always began by saying that I hardly knew what I was talking about, a bit of an exaggeration—or was it? I said I was at the front of the room, conducting the class, because I had read a lot of Baldwin. Then, as if in an aside, I related how I had *heard* Baldwin lecture on the campus in the late Seventies. Moreover, I was able to point out of the window (for almost 30 years the authorities gave me the same classroom for this Prose Fiction course) to the wonderful Stanford White building where Baldwin had spoken. Then I would top that by saying how in the Eighties I had seen Baldwin at the bar of the El Faro Restaurant in the West Village; and how I had actually gone up to him and told him I was having trouble getting copies of *Going to Meet the Man* (the book we were reading in that class). He replied, "That's why I'm here now in New York." Talk about touching the hand that touched the hand.

I also shared with the class that I was old enough to have seen the legally segregated South, telling them how, while in college in 1956, I had travelled with some pals through the South. I had witnessed the "White Only" and "Colored Only" signs; I had seen how at the racetrack Black people had to sit in a segregated section farthest from the finish line. I told them how I had visited New Orleans to hear classic Black jazz musicians; how in a small place, called the Paddock Lounge, I sat during a break at the bar next to the leader of the band, a noted trombonist named Bill Matthews. I asked him if one of my friends, a terrific trumpet player, could sit in for one number. Matthews looked at me and said it was impossible, that the bar owner would lose his license, that in the state of Louisiana white and Black performers were forbidden to appear together on the same stage. The students seemed to acknowledge that, although I was a white man, I did know a little about the experience of Black people and was concerned with civil rights.

In any event, during a discussion of Baldwin, I was making the case that some strides towards racial justice had been made during the Sixties, that is, after the days in which Baldwin's stories were set. Apparently, the class agreed. But then a young man, in the front row to my right, stood up and insisted that nothing had really changed, that Black people were as oppressed as ever, and that here in the North racism, though hidden, was as bad as in the South. I of course would not contradict him, and for a moment silence reigned. Then from the back row to my left, an older woman, who could have been the young man's mother or grandmother, stood up and looked across at him and said, "Oh son, you're too young. You don't know what you're talking about. You don't know what it was like back then, but I do. I lived through it." He made no reply, nor did anyone else speak up. I could have kissed her.

Another white-teacher-Black-student moment came when a student, who for most of the semester had sat quietly in the back of the room, raised his hand, and said that I seemed "pretty good with Black people" and asked how had I come to that. I told him I grew up in the Forties in a rural all-white neighborhood in New Jersey; and how I was a member of a gang of little kids who were all fanatic Brooklyn Dodger fans; and that when Jackie Robinson came to the team we loved him. True, and not a bad answer, if I say so who should not.

But who knows if he or she as a teacher is really doing any good? We don't know and can only relish a few good memories. I recall one *very* good moment, when the Department Chair told me that at the previous year's commencement, the student valedictorian, a Latina, had listed things the college had done for her, one of which was "Professor Hall taught me to think." Granted that's one out of an estimated 4,000 students who passed through my classes, but I'll take it.

COME, MY AGNOSTIC FRIENDS

AGNOSTICISM IS OFTEN a timid position, the mark of a person afraid to take a stand, afraid to oppose the general drift of the public's thinking (or that of his or her family or tribe), afraid of looking evidence and reality squarely in the face. I concede that there exist many true agnostics, perplexed or troubled souls who cannot fully embrace either theism or atheism. I was once such myself, and I quote my own words about the state of my mind as a freshman in college:

> Back in 1951 I was trying to balance unbelief, the result of too much thinking about the gratuitous assumptions behind religious thought, against belief, ingrained over many years and bolstered by the everyday realities of the religious atmosphere in which I moved. Without ever having heard of John Keats' "Negative Capability," I was in fact straining for it, the art of remaining "in uncertainties, mysteries, doubts, without any irritable reaching after fact and reason," the art of negating the logical, rational part of the mind and being content with "half knowledge." Of course I was still reaching after fact and reason.

For these honest agnostics I can express only sympathy and hope that they may eventually resolve the question. My own case, complicated by my being wedded to Catholicism as a seminarian and later as a priest, took me *fifteen years* to unravel. (That struggle eventually formed the basis for a memoir, *Belief*, Beil, 2007.) On the other hand, my concern here is those other agnostics, individuals who really ought to know better, but who for various reasons prefer to shelter behind excuses. Four of these come to mind: 1/ The I-can't-be-bothered attitude towards things thought to be beyond reach or usefulness, matters sometimes termed "metaphysical" or "mysterious." 2/ A vague "philosophical" sense of not being able to prove a negative. 3/ A feeling of not wanting to stand out (in a bad sense) and be associated with "atheism," a word that has forever had the nastiest of reputations. 4/ A misplaced sense of impartiality, of giving believers or their beliefs a fair hearing.

Before musing on these excuses, I must assert that this brief essay will make no attempt to sway believers. That way madness lies. It's largely a case of rational thought vs irrational belief—and the rational folks have no chance. It's easier to convince a Pittsburgh Pirates fan to become a Yankee lover. I am, however, just foolish enough to think one might argue sensibly (although with admittedly little hope of success) the case for moving from agnosticism to atheism. The argument slips toward the existence-of-god question, an issue which cannot be divorced from the discussion of agnosticism. I also admit that I am presuming the non-existence of god as a fact, the very item that is at the center of the question; my excuse is that I see agnostics as already more than half-way home. So here goes—some thoughts on the reticence of certain agnostics to take the final step:

1/ Rather than pronounce oneself an atheist, and not wanting to challenge the belief of almost the entire country, isn't it easier to declare that the existence of god and the reality of an afterlife are "transcendental" and "mysterious" questions? And that as such they are simply beyond us? So, why trouble? Why? Because reality matters. To say belief in a creator-god and an afterlife are "transcendental" issues that we should not mess with is nonsense. These questions do not fly over our heads, they are not beyond us, they do not transcend us; they are readily addressed and answered, elsewhere (see Richard Dawkins or Christopher Hitchens). But how about mysteriousness? Surely countless phenomena are truly mysterious, beginning with why there is something rather than nothing, down to countless smaller mysteries of the universe and of everyday life. But other so-called mysteries, like the existence of god, are not in fact mysteries at all; they are rooted in clearly mistaken premises, or meaningless, good old-fashioned ignorance. They cannot be solved—any more than the mysteries of astrology can be solved—because the mysteries are not there in the first place. We cannot understand such fantasies because there is nothing to understand. An all-too-obvious instance is the Trinity in the Roman Catholic tradition. But the absurdity of the Trinity rests on a foundation of a still greater "non-mystery," viz., the existence of an imaginary supreme creator. The only real mystery is that so many people still believe in some kind of god.

2/ Right, you cannot prove a negative. Here Bertrand Russell's famous counter-argument remains valid: if someone asserts that there is a teapot somewhere between Earth and Mars circling the sun, no one could or need disprove him; the burden of proof is on the teapot believer; and the belief in it is nonsense, "unfalsifiable" nonsense that need not be disproved, even when bolstered by some ancient books.

3/ Agreed. It is often unpleasant or worse to buck the world's general opinion, as, say Copernicus and Galileo famously did, even if one is convinced, and rightly so, that his opinion is true. And, yes, atheists—in this country, certainly—are looked on as little short of felons. Would that we had a better word for atheism. But religions, those primitive superstitions and crude explanations for the way things are, have so long held the field that believers in evidence, in rational thought, in science, in things as they are, have to be labeled in a negative manner, as in the very word "atheist" ("a" being Greek "not"). It's the same for the alternative term "non-believer." Indeed even the word "skeptic" arises from a negative context. Till the right word comes along, we are atheists, sad as that word is. We might as well call all decently behaving men "non-rapists."

4/ True it is that most good and sincere people the world over believe in some god or other. Why not—almost out of kindness—give these believers a break and allow that they just may be right? You might just as well give the same benefit of the doubt to those who formerly believed in Jupiter, Zeus, Ra, or Thor, or who insisted that the sun goes around the Earth. No, I think theism should be given no quarter, even though society condemns (unofficially but powerfully) any attack on or—god forbid—making fun of, religious beliefs. Everything else is fair game; we can attack fascism and vaccine hesitancy, but we must refrain from any criticism of laughable, preposterous, religious beliefs. Hold on, I hear. *Belief*, that's the key word. We theists only *believe* in a God; we are willing to admit that we do not strictly *know* that God exists. Please, stop the word games. Do I only *believe* that there will be daylight tomorrow or do I *know* it? I know it for all practical purposes and for all theoretical purposes. I know it or I believe I know it, if you will. Makes no difference. We each of us know damn well what we mean here, and to fall back on the belief-vs-knowledge dodge is as good as to admit defeat. This pious tactic is sometimes worded as positing religious faith as "belief in things unseen." Like the guardian angel by my side, assigned by the Creator to guide and protect me. You can't see the angel because he or she is a spirit. Sillier even than Russell's teacup.

Come, my fellow doubters, free-thinkers, skeptics, rationalists, my agnostic cousins, stand up and be counted. 'Tis not too late to seek a newer world. Say after me, "Oh God, I do not believe. Help Thou my unbelief." Atheism may not be as warm, as comforting, as inspiring as religion. All atheism has on its side, all that can be said for it, is that it fits the facts. For many, this facticity (or truth) is nasty, bewildering, disenchanting. I don't think it need be perceived this way. But be that as it may, it is the way things are. Any takers?

GODDAM RIGHT

IN A RECENT POST, I argued that the word *enormity* should be restricted to a single meaning. Here I shall do an about-face and look at the myriad meanings and implications of the word *goddam* and its affiliates *damn* and *God damn it (you, him,* etc). You can do this with countless words, but I find this one especially ripe with nuance. (I resist the temptation to examine the contextual possibilities of the constituent word *god:* godawful, godforsaken, god-fearing, godlike, god-given, godless, godly, godsend, god-sent; and innumerable expressions: God! Oh God! Oh my God! God Almighty! By God, God in heaven, Thank God, For God's sake, In God's name, Ye gods and little fishes, God's acre, God's country, God knows, God's gift, God's plenty, God's truth, God willing, God forbid, God help us!)

This ubiquitous word goddam (adjective, noun, verb, expletive), together with its shorter and longer versions, is now nowhere near as shocking as previously. The word qualifies as slangy and a bit profane; and for children it still comes under the category of a "bad word." It may be vulgar, but it is not regarded as sacrilegious or blasphemous. It's an old "swear word," and a "curse" only in a mild, broad, even ironic, sense. And its use is not considered "taking God's name in vain." Note the small "g," and the diluted "damn." The word has strayed far from its meaning of asking the all-just God to damn someone to a hell of eternal suffering. And "God damn it" would make no sense if we took it in the old-fashioned literal sense, because, as the scriptures tell us, the all-loving God damns only *humans* to hell, not abstractions or situations or books or theories or cats or dogs.

Let's look at *goddam* in various contexts, and, in a kind of mental exercise, ask ourselves its meanings in the following:

>I hurt my goddam knee.
>I don't give a good goddam.
>Goddam it all.
>I'm feeling pretty goddam tired.
>I failed the goddam exam.
>I lost my goddam temper.
>I can't find my goddam hearing aids.
>She was awfully goddam pretty.
>Please don't crash my goddam Tesla.
>I just won the goddam lottery.
>I got an *A* on the goddam test.
>He's a goddam moron.
>You're goddam right.

Moreover, try the same exercise with the simple *damn:*

>That's damn nice of you.
>Who gives a damn?
>He damn near killed me.
>Damned if I know.
>He's a damn fool.

These examples, with their different denotations, are everyday and prosaic. Let's also look at some *loci classici* in the written word. Exhibit number one could be Harold Ross, founding editor and guiding genius of the *New Yorker* for its first 25 years. In a beguiling study of the man, *The Years with Ross,* 1959, James Thurber posits "Ross's virtual inability to talk without a continuous flow of profanity," a profanity which "formed the skeleton of his speech, the very foundation of his manner and matter." Thurber believes that Ross was "never actually conscious of his profanity," and that without it he would have been tongue-tied." Ross' *goddam* "referred to a god that had nothing to do with the Deity."

Here are a few goddam instances from the inimitable Harold Ross: He tells Thurber, "Everybody thinks he knows English. But nobody does. I think it is because of the goddam women schoolteachers." Ross' mother was a schoolteacher. When staff writer John McNulty left the magazine for Hollywood, a sorrowing Ross closes his goodbye letter, "Well, God bless you, McNulty, goddam it." (I recommend McNulty's short morality tale in the *New Yorker* titled "Atheist Hit by Truck.") When Thurber was in the hospital for an eye operation—in 1940, during the time of the German blitz—Ross came over to his bed and snarled, "Goddam it, Thurber, I worry about you and England." Ross, always nervous about the slightest hint of sex connected to anyone on his magazine, told Thurber that he had noticed a woman staff-writer at dinner: "Last night, at Tony's, she was damn near sitting in the lap of the man she was with." But Thurber, who had also been in the restaurant, protests that the two were just sitting and talking like any other couple. To which Ross says, "They were talking in awful goddam low tones." Thurber, adopting his boss' style, modifies Shakespeare, "Her voice was gentle and goddam low, an excellent thing in a woman." Ross replies, "Goddam it, Thurber, don't quote things at me."

Continually lamenting the lack of humor in his magazine's fiction, Ross said, "If a man in these goddam grim stories doesn't shoot his wife, he shoots himself." When Ross' only child was born a girl, he was at first troubled and said things such as, "Goddam it, I don't like the idea of going around with female hormones in me." Visiting

Paris, he wouldn't go to Sainte Chapelle: "Stained glass is damned embarrassing." And it was also "goddam embarrassing" for Thurber to send him, even as a joke, red roses on his birthday.

Ross typically uses the word with a sense of annoyance or complaint. For more variation we can look to another great godammer, who appeared on the American scene about the time of Ross' death in 1951. Holden Caulfield, a fictitious character but "real" to millions of readers, is a teenager for whom the word *goddam* also formed the skeleton and basis of his speech. I'll quote a handful of instances from the first part of *The Catcher in the Rye*. When Holden is still at Pencey Prep, but about to run off, he tells the reader, "I was the goddam manager of the fencing team. Very big deal. I left all the foils and the equipment and stuff on the goddam subway." He tells a teacher about a former school, Elkton Hills, where he "was surrounded by phonies.... They were coming in the goddam window.... I hated that goddam Elkton Hills." He relates how a rich alumnus visits the campus in "this big goddam Cadillac." Holden says of his roommate Stadlater that he has big "goddam shoulders" and "was forever combing his goddam gorgeous hair.... He spent around half of his goddam life in front of the mirror."

But among the hundreds of goddam sentences in the novel, my favorites involve Holden's next-door roommate, Robert Ackley, whom Holden is always calling "Ackley kid." Ackley hates it when Holden calls him that:

> "Stop calling me 'Ackley kid,' God damn it. I'm old enough to be your lousy father."
> "No you are not.... In the first place I wouldn't let you *in* my goddam family."

In another exchange, Holden, having awakened Ackley, whom he knew to be a Catholic, asks him if you have to be a Catholic to join a monastery:

"*Cer*tainly, you have to be a Catholic. You bastard, did you wake me up just to ask me a dumb..."

"Ah, go back to sleep. The kind of luck I have, I'd probably join one with all the wrong kind of monks in it. All stupid bastards. Or just bastards."

"Listen, I don't care what you say about me or anything, but if you start making cracks about my goddam *religion*, for Chrissake—"

"Nobody's making cracks about your goddam religion."

And so on. That's just a few of the novel's 245 *goddams* (they contributed to the removal of the book from many school libraries). But these examples are enough to suggest some of the delicious nuance this word can carry. One especially strikes my fancy. Holden is trying to read Isak Dinesen's *Out of Africa*, but Ackley keeps standing in his "goddam light" and interrupting him, refusing to take the "goddam hint" and let him read in peace:

> Ackley: "What the hellya reading?"
> Holden: "Goddam book."

COMEDY: AN APOLOGIA

ROB POLHEMUS, who happens to be a friend of mine, was for many years chairman of the English department at Stanford (on the West Coast, Harvard is known as the Stanford of the East). He has written half-a-dozen important books, and I'd like to comment here on one of them, *Comic Faith: The Great Tradition from Austen to Joyce*. There are countless works on comedy, satire, wit, humor, parody, laughter, and they amount to a morass of contradictions, finding comedy saintly and worldly, liberal and conservative, subversive of the status quo and fostering of it, sympathetic and hostile, therapeutic and dissipating. But I'll focus on Polhemus, and limit myself to laying out his general thesis, without going into his applications of it to various classic English novels. (I will throw in my two cents here and there.) Polhemus argues for the existence in modern life and literature of what he calls "comic faith," this faith consisting of, among other things, a belief that the world is "both funny and potentially good" and that comedy expresses itself through "religious impulses, motives, and meanings."

The first belief we must take, excuse the expression, on faith. The second is the heart of his thesis, namely, that works of comedy, here novels, when read in the right frame of mind, can help satisfy human yearnings that in times past were addressed (and to some degree assuaged) by religion. He is not naïve enough to think that comic faith will replace nearly universal religious belief, but he suggests that it can perform some of the offices hitherto reserved for religion. This sounds like a big order, but please give him a listen. God knows we have listened long enough to the proponents, peddlers if you will, of religious doctrines and arguments. Hear him out. First, he lists what he considers the main purposes of religion:

> to honor creation;
> to provide hope;
> to reconcile people to their harsh fates;
> to smooth over social enmity and to defend culture by authoritative moral sanction against selfish and destructive behavior;
> to make people feel important, part of a "chosen" group;
> to institutionalize ways of getting rid of guilt;
> to allow people to identify with righteousness and let loose wrathful indignation and hostility in good conscience;
> to assure them of the possibility of future well-being; to lift them out of themselves, to free their spirits.

It's a curious list—no mention of a god—but it sets forth goals that religious people and those who know the inside of religious communities will, I think, agree are among the foremost purposes of religion. And, Polhemus argues, these are the purposes—*mutatis mutandis*—of literary comedy. Comic novels, if we share his approach, can imaginatively serve these functions while offering a temporary balm, some partial cessation from life's worries and sufferings. Of course, by comedy he doesn't mean just stories that are "funny" and have a "happy ending." He means narratives which give emphasis to the good things of this world, which focus sharply on the here-and-now and not some hoped-for afterlife or utopia; he means fictions that celebrate life, that endorse and suggest pleasure, love in its various forms, especially sexual love, charm, time-off from rules; the delights of eating, drinking, singing, dancing, joking, laughing, socializing; triumphing over transitory sorrows, while at the same time mocking the pretentions and self-importance of the spoil-sports, kill-joys, and Puritans, all the self-appointed guardians of virtue and morality. Comic faith is a world view, a *Weltanschauung*.

To come to a particular instance of the comedy/religion analogy: as prayer is a vital part of religion, so laughter is in comedy. Orthodox religions have historically demonized laughter. Polhemus quotes Ecclesiastes, "I said of laughter, it is mad; and of mirth, what doeth it?" and that "the heart of fools is in the house of mirth." But Polhemus will have none of this: "If we compare comic euphoria with religious ecstasy, we readily see the ties between mirth and religious emotions; both often manifest themselves in states of rapt bliss in which people become oblivious of the ordinary circumstances and concerns of passing life." While most religions try to belittle "experiences other than worship and belief and reliance on a god outside of our material world," comic faith echoes another sentence from Ecclesiastes, that enigmatic book: "Then, I commended mirth, because a man hath no better things under the sun than to eat, drink, and be merry."

Again, "Institutional religion seeks immortality by offering an afterlife; the comic sense works by momentarily purging the mind of unpleasant contents—the consciousness that 'I am a creature who must die.' Comic laughter produces within us a surge of pure life uncontaminated by Thanatos." But intense comic pleasure cannot be long sustained, and if we are not careful, traditional religions with their promise of eternal life "will obscure the life-enhancing role of comedy." You may object that Polhemus is presenting comic novels as simply a distraction from the actual sad state of things, something that tragic novels do just as well. No. Tragic novels do distract us and give some surcease from everyday troubles and concerns, but comedy offers a different kind of relief. Comedy may not be as sublime, as terrifying, as "grand" as tragedy, but it is positive and heartening; it amuses, charms, and delights. And we need that. I call on no less an authority than James Joyce, who, referring to Aristotle's famous dictum on the cathartic value of tragedy as releasing us from the arousal of pity and fear, insisted that "Comedy makes for joy, while tragedy makes for sorrow; the sense of possession of joy in the one being superior to the sense of deprivation in the other." Not a majority view, but one well worth considering.

Enough. I am not doing justice to Polhemus' argument. But I will mention one more issue he raises: "In the culture of male supremacy, comedy, relatively speaking, has a built-in feminist bias. It deals with generational matters and the relations of the sexes, and, in matters of the heart, to say nothing of reproduction, the sexes are equally concerned. Comedy is strongest just where religion is weakest." Indeed, sex is something religions have for the most part gotten egregiously wrong: not only by inflicting useless guilt, but chiefly by debasing women, sometimes relegating them to almost subhuman status. (There is also in Christianity, the honoring, one might say the worshipping, of virginity over motherhood—a truly "unnatural" and ridiculous stance.) George Meredith, whom Polhemus would have done well to bring in here, writes: "There is no comedy in the East because of the veil over the woman's face; there may be fun in Baghdad but not comedy, no real civilization—that comes of some degree of equality between the sexes; where women are on the road to equality with men, comedy flourishes." (Meredith, like J S Mill, qualifies as that elusive figure, the male feminist; he also advocated, among other radical views, five-year contracts for marriage, something said to have kept him, on his death in 1909, out of Poets' Corner in Westminster Abbey.)

So, think about reading the great classic comic novels—they are far more rare than the great tragic ones. Zero in on Jane Austen, much of Dickens, Thackeray's *Vanity Fair* (arguably the greatest comic novel in the language), numerous Trollope novels, Mrs Gaskell's

Wives and Daughters, Lewis Carrol's Alice books, Hardy's *Under the Greenwood Tree*, Butler's *The Way of All Flesh*, and yes, Joyce's *Ulysses* and *Finnegans Wake*.

Polhemus' Introduction closes:

> Hannah Arendt quotes Berthold Brecht's remark, "One may say that tragedy deals with the sufferings of mankind in a less serious way than comedy." She adds, "This of course is a shocking statement; I think at the same time that it is entirely true." They mean, I think, that comic vision does not give to suffering and to evil a dangerous romantic grandeur or an inevitable dominance. Instead, it makes suffering mean and seeks to transcend it. Comic vision is also very serious about the *joys*, as well as the sufferings, of mankind, more serious in one way than organized religions have often been: growing out of a transitory pleasure, comedy does not disparage or devalue the passing joys and victories in the world. Comic faith seeks something less grandiose and more reasonable than infinite or permanent happiness and blessed immortality: it seeks more joyful life in a lasting world.

This world. Right. We don't need pie in the sky. Earth's the place.

CLICHÉS

ALL THE EXPERTS tell writers to avoid clichés. The *New Yorker* Guide for Editors says, "Anything that you suspect of being a cliché undoubtedly is one and had better be removed." Of course, disagreement abounds about whether a phrase is a cliché, because one man's Mede is another man's Persian, just as one man's meat is another man's poison. But it's best to start with a definition, like this one from *Fowler's Modern English Usage*: "A stereotype... a phrase whose felicity in a particular context when it was first employed has won so much popularity that it is apt to be used unsuitably and indiscriminately." (Note that the word cliché itself is invariably pejorative.) Clichés, then, are combinations of words that, after a once brilliant coupling, have with overuse become deadly to writing. Moreover, if we do occasionally feel compelled to use them, we must remain aware that many clichés are metaphors and metaphors usually should not be "mixed."

The same *Fowler's*—a work revered for its precision and despised for its authoritarianism—offers examples: *filthy lucre; sleep the sleep of the just; suffer a sea change; leave no stone unturned; acid test; a blessing in disguise; blissful ignorance; an aching void; conspicuous by his absence; a consummation devoutly to be wished; damn with faint praise; explore every avenue; the fair sex; few and far between; free gratis and for nothing; a hardy annual; the inner man; cherished beliefs; daughter of Eve; irony of fate; last but not least; method in his madness; more in sorrow than in anger; more sinned against than sinning; neither rhyme nor reason; splendid isolation; of that ilk; the powers that be; shake the dust from off one's feet; tender mercies; sound sleep; there's the rub; to be or not to be; through thick and thin; tower of strength; wheels within wheels.*

Fowler says of such clichés that if a writer as much as *thinks* about using them he or she must "beware of perpetuating bad writing." That these clichés are drawn from lists published in 1965, with some going back to the first edition of 1926, suggests that clichés—except for a few not repeated here, like the British "own the soft impeachment" and "curate's egg"—are holding up nicely. Furthermore, we recognize many as coming from celebrated lines in literature. I remember seeing Richard Burton in *Hamlet* on Broadway in 1964, and during the interval hearing someone in the lobby say "… And all the quotations!"

For a more up-to-date take on clichés, we find the Web giving numerous examples (one site offers "681 clichés"). Notice again that many arise from literature and end up proverbial: *a bed of roses; a bolt from the blue; a bull in a China shop; play your cards right; read between the lines; an uphill battle; better safe than sorry; don't judge a book by its cover; the grass is always greener; a chip off the old block; a dead ringer; a diamond in the rough; a drop in the bucket; a dish fit for the gods; a fate worse than death; a fish out of water; a fly in the ointment; a fool's paradise; a friend in need; a frog in my throat; a good man is hard to find; a half-baked idea; a horse of a different color; a jack of all trades; a knight in shining armor; a labor of love; a legend in one's own time; a leopard doesn't change its spots; a little bird told me; a multitude of sins; a necessary evil; a man after my own heart; a new lease on life; a picture is worth a thousand words; a plague on both your houses; a riddle wrapped up in an enigma; a shoestring budget; a shot in the dark; a shotgun wedding; a sight for sore eyes; a stone's throw away; a sweet deal; a taste of his own medicine; a thorn in the flesh; a watched pot never boils; an ace in the hole; an ace up his sleeve; airing dirty laundry in public; all bent out of shape; all bets are off; all hands on deck; all hell breaks loose; all in a day's work; all in due time; all over the map; all talk and no action.*

Wow. Additionally, some authorities hold that single words can exuberate into clichés; I myself would label such words "fancy" or "literary" or "vogue." There is nothing wrong with any word (except atrocities like "irregardless" and "discombobulated"). It's always context: ameliorate vs improve; beverage vs drink; bodeful vs ominous; comestibles vs food; dubiety vs doubt; edifice vs building; envisage vs foresee; feasible vs possible; function vs work; initiate vs begin; partake vs share; perchance vs perhaps; peruse vs read; reside vs live; slumber vs sleep. (My own favorite stylish words include "thereanent" and "apodictic," along with some English clichés that have quickly arrived in the U. S., like "spot on" and "funnily enough.") Context, as I say, is everything: *Let's get some comestibles and beverages and later slumber*. We must also beware of the suffix "wise"— a four letter word that can ruin almost any noun: "The used car was pricewise a bargain."

But, on the other hand, easy as it is to find fault with clichés and pretentious words, here are some second thoughts. No less a master than Max Beerbohm eulogized Lytton Strachey, whom he considered the supreme prose writer of his day, saying that Strachey "is not even afraid of clichés." And Fowler himself, that staunch believer in a pure, simple, "correct" English style, says that while we rightly abhor certain age-old clichés *(filthy lucre, sleep the sleep of the just, tender mercies, leave no stone unturned)*, we should nevertheless recognize that some clichés are valuable and even necessary; Fowler asks whether writers are never to be allowed to use *foregone conclusion, Hobson's choice, white elephant, feather his nest, tongue in cheek, bee in his bonnet*. He observes that "What is new is not necessarily better than what is old; the original felicity that has made the phrase a cliché may not be beyond recapture." Fowler goes on to say that the really well-worn clichés *(filthy lucre, no stone unturned, etc)* are not what chiefly tempt writers into a "lazy acceptance of a prefabricated phrase"; rather, the real problem comes with insidious or innocent phrases that, almost unnoticed, are on the way to becoming clichés, often by unnecessary expansion: "climate of opinion"; "within the framework"; "grinding to a halt"; "in this day and age"; "in the last analysis." One thinks today of "at this point in time" and "It's in our DNA."

Oh my, exhausted? Clichés are a huge and confounding subject. The problem perdures (another precious word). What are we to do? Can we take any action other than the sometimes impractical one, as expressed in another cliché, namely, "to avoid them like the plague"? Well, we should remember first that context counts more than anything else. Then, we can employ some tactics: use clichés and vogue words humorously; or, put the words in quotation marks. Another dodge is attaching phrases like "as they say" or "as the youngsters say." But, at bottom (I was about to say *au fond* but won't because using foreign words when a good English equivalent exists is its own kind of cliché), it all comes down to staying careful.

If we want to sleep the sleep of the just, that is to say—not to put too fine a point on it—if we want to keep our house or domicile or residence or place of habitation in order, if we want to keep our powder dry, and not fall asleep at the switch in this matter of words (including being ever on the *qui vive* in regard to foreign tongues), if we don't want to be up the creek with no light at the end of the tunnel, it behooves us in this day and age and at this point in time, authorshipwise, to practice, practice, practice—because practice makes perfect—namely, and to wit, we must practice a vigilance more than quotidian or diurnal or eternal or even sempiternal. At the same time and simultaneously let us pray withal that the good Lord above will mercifully and hopefully grant that our quest for the aforementioned vigilance—specifically in the area of inquisitiveness into the feasibility of the usefulness or non-usefulness of these problematic clichés and fancy words—let us pray that this our quest for vigilance go from strength to strength, and not, heaven forfend, at close of day, and when all is said and done, lose force, dwindle, or end altogether in a whimper or a bang; let us implore the Almighty that our worst literary forebodings come not home to roost, that we not find ourselves, in the long run, in a type of *cul de sac* or a dead end situation that may or may not resemble or equate with a fine kettle of fish, a dog's breakfast, or a can of worms surpassing any rabbit's hole; but, rather, may we *mais oui* keep ourselves, in this vale of tears, actually, and to all intents and purposes, totally, and always, up in arms, up and at 'em, fighting the good fight; for unless, to reiterate again, we remain steadfast in an anti-cliché mode, in a perpetual watchfulness, we may witness our hopes for a pleasant style in writing, if not exactly disappearing into thin air, or going down the tubes, or down the drain, but, nearly as bad, being decimated and landing us not in the promised land of milk and honey and publication and just about everything else including the kitchen sink, but in a desert, a stale and unprofitable place, barren except for a surfeit of hackneyed, well-worn, bankrupt phrases and etceteras.

THE CHURCH & SEXUAL SIN: PART I

RELIGIONS HAVE, for the most part, screwed up when it comes to sex: think guilt, degradation of women, abhorrence and persecution of homosexuality. I'm no expert on other religions but I do know something about the Roman Catholic Church and sex in the 1940s, 1950s, and 1960s. Indeed, I know more than is, or was, good for me. Here, like an old divine, I shall divide my sermon into two parts, the comic and the tragic. The comic draws on six years of "higher education" in the seminary; the tragic draws on my eight years as a parish priest.

The Immaculate Conception Seminary (a wonderful name for the "seed time" place of preparing men for the priesthood) was my home, or perhaps my house of detention, from 1953 through 1959, *aetat* 20-26. For many, these are "the best years of our lives" (a fellow seminarian commented "Yes, and that is the damn of it all"). But for myself and my fellow inmates, our early twenties were spent being indoctrinated with Catholic catechism. Sex was central to much of what we were taught in "Moral theology" (equal in importance to "Dogmatic theology"). This emphasis on sexual sin may surprise you, or maybe not.

But first, the setting: Darlington, as the seminary was also called, was located on 1,400 bucolic acres in the wilds of northwestern New

Jersey—miles from any town or village, i.e., cut off from "the world," most notably from women. Women, especially young or youngish women, were seen as the enemy, the possible cause of defection from the seminarian's holy vocation; women were so alien to us that we were tempted to think of them as almost a different species. This phenomenon prompts me to mention a small event that nonetheless points a moral: The rector, Monsignor Joseph Brady, a severe and unyielding tyrant, once, in a mysterious lapse, hired a young woman as secretary in the ground floor office of the classroom building (hundreds of yards distant from the dormitory/refectory/chapel building). A woman on the grounds! She worked there only a few months, and I forget her name, but I recall various seminarians finding some excuse to visit the office, merely to have a look at a woman.

The key to the Church's teaching in regard to sex was that sins of impurity—taking pleasure in illicit sexual activity, whether physical or mental—admitted no *parvity*, no smallness, of matter. Sexual transgressions were *per se* mortally sinful, and mortal sin boded punishment of burning in hell for eternity. (How could any half-intelligent persons—even youths in their early twenties—have subscribed to this nonsense? Children have their Santa Claus, their Tooth Fairy, their Easter Bunny, for sure, and good for them. But grownups?) A sexual sin could be venial, small, only in the case of an action that constituted a slight "occasion of sin," namely, putting oneself *in danger of* committing a sin. Thus, our moral theology professor, Al Welsh—himself extra strict in regard to "purity"—held that it was "at *least* a venial sin" to read the *Daily News* three days running, because of the girlie pictures featured on that paper's third page. (To dwell on the photographs "and take mental pleasure" in them was a mortal sin.) His argument was undercut when it was learned that the newly-appointed Spiritual Director of the Seminary, old Monsignor George "Wee Bonnie" Baker, had the *Daily News* delivered to his room every day. But Welsh, despite this apparent setback, would not compromise with absolute prohibitions. How, for example, might a married man collect his sperm to have it tested for fertility? Masturbation was out of the question, as was the use of a condom. Solution: the man and his wife should, under the auspices of a doctor, be supplied with a room near the laboratory, where they would have sex using a *perforated* condom, which, it was to be hoped, would catch enough of the sperm for medical evaluation, while still allowing the act of sex its "natural" purpose of depositing sperm into the vagina, for possible "procreation."

Our textbook, *De Sexto* ("Concerning the Sixth Commandment"), the work of a man named Hieronymus Noldin, remained—unlike other theology manuals—in "the decent obscurity of the Latin tongue." In English it might have been too explicit. Happily enough, in 1955 there appeared in translation a book on moral theology by one Heribert Jone, and this curious work became a kind of *vade mecum*—a guide as to moral teachings for us aspiring priests. I still own that invaluable volume and will quote from it to document what I am saying here, lest you think I exaggerate.

The foundation is simply put: "All directly voluntary sexual pleasure [mental or physical] outside of marriage is mortally sinful. This is true even if the pleasure is ever so brief and insignificant."

Solitary sexual sins: Topping that list was masturbation, referred to as "self-abuse," or, Jone's preferred term, "pollution." A trickier area was mental sins of impure thoughts or desires, mortally sinful always if one "took pleasure" in the thought or desire. You can imagine the possibilities here. An interesting subdivision is that of *delectatio morosa*, "morose delectation," defined as "The deliberate complacency in a sinful object presented to the imagination":

> The forbidden character of morose delectation remains even though the object will later become lawful or if it was formerly lawful: Engaged persons, therefore, may not

imagine their future marital relationships as present and take pleasure in them. The same may be said of the widowed concerning past marital relations.

Mortal sin can arise from reading "obscene" books. To read novels by authors listed by name in the *Index of Prohibited Books* was not only gravely sinful but incurred *ipso facto* (automatically, with ignorance of the law as no excuse) excommunication. Some examples: Stendhal, Balzac, Dumas père and fils, Flaubert, Sand, Hugo, Zola (to name only some 19th-century French novelists). Jone does offer a qualification: If the danger of "contamination" were remote, one could get by with reading 30 pages and commit only a venial sin, but if the book were very obscene "even half a page may be sufficient to constitute a mortal sin ... To retain forbidden books is a mortal sin if one keeps them for more than a month. But it is not sinful to keep a such a book for a short time because one intends to surrender it to the authorities." So, some of you readers might unawares have been excommunicated for reading *Madame Bovary*.

Under the heading of Modesty, we are given warnings about touches:

> For a reasonable cause one may touch even the indecent parts [!] of his own person (e.g., for bathing). Without sufficient reason such touches are at most venial sins if one knows that he will not be sexually excited thereby. Should one without a reason continue these actions for a length of time he will usually experience sexual excitement; wherefore such actions can readily become grave sins. For pedagogical reasons children should be taught to refrain from such touches entirely.

How about that last for advice on parenting?

As for touching someone other than oneself:

> It is seriously sinful to touch the indecent parts of others (even over the clothing) without a reason, regardless of sex. Such touches are venially sinful only when done without an evil intention and in a hasty or casual manner or out of levity or in jest. Touching the less decent parts [the buttocks? not as "indecent" as the genitals?] of a person of the same sex is generally a venial sin at most, whereas it is usually a grave sin in the case of the opposite sex.

And while we are at it: "Touching animals indecently is generally not gravely sinful unless it is done with the evil intention or for a long time or until the animal suffers pollution." Additionally, "It is venially sinful out of curiosity to observe animals mating if no sexual pleasure is caused."

More on "observing":

> In itself it is not lawful to use women and girls as models with only the genital organs covered [sic]. But if young artists in their training are compelled to attend art academies, they do not sin by sketching such models. They must however not consent to any commotion [ah!] that may arise, and they must try to render the danger remote by prayer and renewal of their good intention.

> If women and girls have no other means to keep them from grave need, they may serve as models, provided they employ the necessary precautionary measures.

> To consider attentively and for a length of time nude pictures and works of art, giving special attention to the genitals, may easily become a serious sin, especially if they are modern works that are made to arouse sensuality.

It was good to have that cleared up, especially in a seminary where the authorities doctored library art books by covering the "indecent" parts of nudes with white paint—"diapers" we called these safeguards.

Next, we have sins with others:

> Decent kissing and embracing as customarily done as a sign of politeness, friendship, relationship, or honorable love are lawful even between persons of the opposite sex, but always on the condition that these actions are not done to excite sexual pleasure. [So be careful kissing your mother-in-law.] Ardent, prolonged, and repeated kissing is often a mortal sin. Not so, however, would be such kissing and embracing between parents and children.

Who dares say the Catholic Church was too strict in matters sexual? You can read right there in black and white: it's perfectly okay for parents to hug their children.

But "Sexual contact of any kind between two people unless married is mortally sinful. Engaged persons are forbidden to do anything which is not permitted to other single people." The latter of course could do next to nothing—although they might dance if properly separated and provided no "commotion" were aroused. Engaged couples should "as far as possible, avoid being alone; neither should they meet too often."

As for married folks, there's no doubt who is in control: "The husband [by marriage] receives *domestic and paternal authority*. The wife has the *obligation to obey* him and the *right to his protection and support.*" As for marital intercourse (to begin with a concession): "Sexual relations are lawful at any time, although during seasons of penance [Lent], temperance is advisable,—it is even lawful the night before going to Holy Communion." That's a relief.

On the vexed question of whether one spouse sins by not obliging the other's (usually the husband's) request for "the marriage debt," we read that refusal is a grave sin. The basic guideline is: "Wives should beware of fulfilling their obligation grudgingly." Jone offers advice to confessors:

> Elderly women and mothers of many children should generally be left in good faith if they think they sin gravely only when they almost always refuse to render the marriage debt.... In general one should rather recall women's attention to the gravity of their obligation and remind husbands to be moderate.

As you can see, the bias in moral theology was decidedly, one might say dismayingly, male. For example, under *Rape*, we read:

> This is a sin against chastity but also against justice; furthermore, a double injury is committed in ravishing a virgin, an unjust violation of her rights and the additional injustice of deflowering her of the possession of physical integrity.... To avoid sinning, a woman who is being ravished must offer internal and external resistance. She need not cry out when this cannot be done without danger to her life or reputation *unless* she would otherwise consent to the sin. Rape is not so common [sic].

You are probably weary of the lunacy, but for the record: Adultery came in two varieties: "imperfect" if the third party were single, and "perfect" adultery if the third party were also married. As for sodomy, that also was divided into perfect and imperfect, perfect being between two men, imperfect being rectal intercourse between a man and a woman. It was a relief to learn that "bestiality (regardless of the animal involved) is the *worst* of all sins of impurity."

So, there's a sampling of what we were taught. I'll close this litany of delights by a quick return to that untranslated and dangerous textbook by Noldin (he is said to have died in an asylum, though this is beside the point, probably). If, in that book you looked in the index and searched out the entry for "Woman," *Mulier,* you found the entry *Vide peccatum,* "See under sin."

THE CHURCH & SEXUAL SIN: PART II

MY PREVIOUS BLOG had fun with the Catholic teachings on sex that were fed to seminarians in the 1950s: diapers inked over the "indecent parts" of old master paintings in art books; perforated condoms for fertility testing; warnings against looking at one's genitals while bathing; the generous concession that parents could hug their children. This follow-up essay will examine some of the damage done by Catholic sexual lunacy as I witnessed it during my eight years as a parish priest, 1959 to 1967. This experience allows me to claim some expertise on the subject. How many of you have heard thousands of confessions? It is no violation of the "seal of confession" to set down some generalizations:

Most boys and young men—and older and married men—repeatedly confessed the sin of "self-abuse," masturbation, and it troubled them and fostered untold guilt.

Most young people of both sexes confessed and worried over "bad thoughts," impure desires, dancing too close, necking, and, especially wicked and damning, "petting." All of which again caused guilt and anxiety.

Engaged couples, who were expected to keep as apart as single persons, were troubled about the same serious sins. Intercourse before marriage was strictly forbidden, but it happened, it actually did. For Catholics the time leading up to the wedding was fraught. Their worries were supposed to end with marriage.

Married partners could have sexual relations—even the night before taking Holy Communion!—provided the sperm was deposited in the "proper receptacle." (Theologians, celibate old white males, simple-minded logic choppers, had at one time debated whether it was permissible for married couples to have sex for pleasure alone and lacking the intention to "procreate"; the more liberal view prevailed and married people, including older people, were allowed to have sex in order to "promote mutual affection" and to relieve the man's—always the man's—troublesome "concupiscence.")

But for married Catholics there remained the intractable and seemingly ever-present problem of birth control. Almost all married couples, at least in the West, practice birth control at some time during their lives together. The only permitted Catholic varieties were abstinence (yes, that was allowed) and the rhythm method (the biggest drawback being that it did not work). But, forbidden under pain of mortal sin were *coitus interruptus*, condoms, uterine devices, and the Pill. People again and again confessed the hideous mortal sin of "unnatural" birth control (although any damned fool not under the Church's spell could have figured out that it was no more "unnatural" than wearing clothes against the cold). People agonized over birth control; it tainted and sometimes ruined their marriage, even their lives. I know. I have had women tell me in confession that their doctor had told them another pregnancy might be fatal: "I am not afraid to die, Father [they were calling 26-year-old me Father], but I don't want to leave my other children without a mother." Can you imagine? And many priests—true to the ludicrous Church teachings—seemed especially called upon to speak out from the pulpit against this "filthy sin." I recall one priest devoting the three

152

talks of the "three hours agony" (the commemoration of Jesus' time on the cross) exclusively to birth control.

Anyone who confessed having had an abortion had to promise to come back the following week because the confessor had to apply to his bishop for the privilege of granting absolution to the anonymous excommunicated "child murderer." (To absolve an ordinary murderer did not require this special dispensation from one's bishop.)

Now for extra-confessional matters: The Church's egregious departure from simple human decency exhibited itself in its treatment of Catholics who married outside the Church, whether in a civil ceremony or, worse, in a Protestant church, or, God forbid, in a synagogue. These renegades were *ipso facto* excommunicated, and their relatives and friends forbidden (usually ineffectively) from as much as attending the wedding. Such bizarre restrictions damaged individuals and sometimes divided families. It was not quite as bad as the shunning practiced in cults like the Jehovah's Witnesses or Scientology, but the similarities are undeniable. (A recent *New Yorker* article reminds us that large successful religions are "cults with time.") Catholics who married outside the Church, even if they had been together for fifty years and had numerous children (considered illegitimate by the Church) and grandchildren, were still only "attempting" marriage.

Divorce was of course inexorably condemned. (The only divorce from a Catholic marriage was by annulment, possible only through large alms to the Church and paying a canon lawyer in Rome to argue the case.) No Catholic could marry a divorced person unless that divorced person had not really been married in the first place because he or she had been only attempting marriage by not marrying in the Church and was thus unmarried and free to marry. (Non-Catholic marriages between non-Catholics were, marvelous to say, deemed valid; it was only when one partner was a straying

Catholic that the ceremony didn't "take." So, if you were going to marry a divorced person, it had better be someone —Catholic or not—from a "bad" marriage.)

It is dismaying that all this repression was perpetrated chiefly by priests of mediocre talents, men who through ordination had been raised to an unimaginably exalted (albeit unearned) position in the eyes of Catholics. These "other Christs" were preaching to their betters about sex; I say "betters" here in that married folk were better informed about sex than were presumably celibate priests. We had been instructed in the seminary that even though we were supposedly innocent about sex, we could direct and instruct on such matters including marriage because "the doctor doesn't have to have cancer to treat it." Most of the clerical marriage advisers had experienced no physical sex other than (most likely) masturbation—aside of course from the child abusers and seducers of their parishioners and sleepers with their housekeepers. I am not making this last bit up. I know. I claim some inside knowledge here. On the other hand, when the Paterson and Newark dioceses (my territory) recently made public the names of the priests defrocked by the Church itself for sexual abuse of children, I was shocked. Many offenders were from the time of my own eight years on the job. I had heard rumors of only one. The cover-up by the bishops was nauseatingly effective. It prompts Juvenal's famous question, *Quis custodiet ipsos custodes*? "Who will guard the guards themselves?"

Another thing, while we are it: Church conservatives try to blame the child abuse on gay priests, but those close to the facts know that almost all the sexual molestations of children were committed by straight men who never grew up emotionally, many of them women-fearing or women-hating.

The Church's hard-line stand against homosexuality is well known. Yet everyone involved knew that many, at least 25 to 30 percent, of Catholic priests and bishops were gay. Good for them. Many of my closest and dearest priest friends were among this number. They were all of course "closeted"; they had to pretend to be straight; or talk themselves into believing they were "bachelor" types. The situation I knew so well continues, and it is dehumanizing, but also blatantly—and hilariously—hypocritical. I think of the cartoon showing the Pope (around 2005, long before Francis) talking to a large audience of priests and bishops and saying that homosexuals would not be permitted to be priests; whereupon the entire room starts to empty, causing the Pope to cry out, "I meant from now on."

Enough of past horrors. We are told that the Church today is much changed. There are almost no Catholic schools left to brainwash or frighten children. The vexed issue of birth control has for all practical purposes disappeared; even among the faithful, common sense in this case has superseded ignorance and superstition. Independent studies indicate that Catholics, even in this strangely religious country, practice birth control at the same high rate as others. Moreover, we can now read obscene novels like *Madame Bovary* without fear of excommunication.

Thus, you may be thinking that I am flogging a dead horse. No. First, the damage done to the psyches and to the physical lives of individuals and families was real. The almost incredible nonsense, the strictures, the warnings, the marriage "laws," the excommunications fostered real worry and guilt and they disturbed the lives of our parents and grandparents. We should be aware of past wrongs, just as we should learn about the burning of heretics and witches. The scars of Catholic sexual teachings remain; and the least we can do is not to dismiss or forget them.

Secondly, despite some changes, the Church continues to stick to much of its obsessed anti-sexual teachings including those that still do unimaginable harm. One gross example is places in Africa where the Church's opposition to condoms and "artificial" birth control has for decades furthered the AIDS epidemic, resulting in countless sicknesses and deaths. I don't know if the Church still teaches that any pleasure taken in sexual thought or act outside of marriage is a mortal sin deserving of punishment in the form of burning in hell for all eternity, but I would not be surprised. I hope they are not still frightening children with this imaginary horror, but I would hesitate to bet against it. And there still remains the ostracism, certainly the refusal of Holy Communion, to people "living in sin" by divorce or by marriage outside the Church. Think too of the recent move of the US bishops (the bishops of all people! We know the moral record of that group) trying to deny Communion to President Biden because he, although not personally favoring abortion (a matter touching sex) defends the laws of this country and a woman's right over her own body. (Stephen Colbert suggests the bishops would be wiser not to condemn Biden publicly but simply and quietly move him to another parish.)

Calm down, you say. Who cares what the bishops say? I believe we should care because the pronouncements of this body (doing its best to be more Catholic than the Pope) is shoring up the conservative tendencies in a distressing number of "sheep" among their flock. One hears that most bishops (aside from a few recent appointments by Francis) are notoriously conservative and pro-Trump. No real surprise there. The Catholic Church for centuries has been for the most part radically conservative, supporting slavery, serfdom, misogyny, anti-Semitism, racism generally, religious wars, homophobia, along with monarchy, autocracy, oligarchy, the rich and powerful against the poor; these together with opposition to secular learning, science, social progress, freedom of thought, democracy. A glorious record easily documented.

But the proposed Biden censure has distracted me. My belief is that not a great deal has changed from the bad old days. One looks in vain for any progress on more recent sexual issues:

Married priests? How could it even be imagined—these ordained miracle workers, our priests, who touch the body of Jesus in the Mass every morning, touching … Oh, it's unthinkable.

Gays in the priesthood (aside of course from the colossal numbers already in)? It would be an abomination. Does not the Old Testament explicitly condemn homosexuality? Yes, but if you want to start basing your argument on that frightful collection of barbarisms, how about the fostering of slavery, genocide, and the treatment of wives and daughters as saleable animals?

Gay marriage? Don't ask. The Church remains in the front-line of opposition to this unnatural aberration.

Women in the priesthood? Oh, ye gods and little fishes, please. Religions have almost invariably seen women as second class, human after a fashion, but rather as a kind of subspecies. Consider the three major monotheistic religions. Who would choose to be a woman in Christianity, Conservative Judaism, or Islam? Even the crazy little storefront outfits and ridiculous but dangerous cults know what women are for. Catholicism is quite plain about it: women are created to produce babies and accommodate–in marriage—man's concupiscence and do menial and domestic work as obedient "helpmates" to their lords and masters. You could look it up. I don't believe in using the Bible as evidence or proof of *anything*, but as you know, modern Christianity offers only an abbreviated version of the Ten Commandments. If you look at the one about not "coveting" something of your neighbor's, you find in the Exodus version that the wife comes in second. The first thing not to covet is your neighbor's house, then his wife, then his servants, then his ox, then his ass, then anything else that is his. In Deuteronomy, the wife does come in first, but is lumped together with man's other "goods," male and female slaves, his ox and ass and "anything that belongs to him." That pretty much sums up the place of women in the Church. And that place is certainly not the at the altar. In fact, any question about women being priests in the Catholic Church is a non-starter. The entire idea of womanhood would need to be basically revised. That won't happen soon. The Church, that infallible guide to everything, instructs us (sometimes cunningly, secretly, implicitly) that these daughters of Eve, these causes of all our sufferings and woe, these alluring and dangerous creatures, are meant to help and serve men. Women had better behave themselves and keep away from aspiring to the priesthood and positions of power within the Church. Let them run bingo games and cake sales but not aspire to ministerial functions.

Okay, I have strong feelings on the subject. But the positions I espouse here (unlike, say, my preferences for Puccini or Trollope or Wells Cathedral or red wine or fireplaces) are overwhelmingly evidence-based. How can any rational person not see the sexual repression and nonsense for what it was and still is? How can so many remain so hoodwinked? Easy. Such loyalty, such surrender to the irrational, anti-scientific, anti-factual, is not intellectual. How could it be? Adherence to Catholic teachings is based on emotional loyalties, feelings of belonging tied to family, ethnicity, culture, etc. Such loyalties can be good, but when they fly in the face of decency, common sense, and human progress, they should be resisted. Countering such deep-seated feelings is close to impossible. But let us pray—if you will—that, however slowly, the strictures will be resisted. Let people keep their loyalties to ancient rituals, to glorious religious architecture, art and music, and occasionally some heroic efforts on behalf of the poor, but let us have less of the anti-human doctrines in regard to the basis of life. From Catholic teaching and attitudes on sex and marriage, oh Lord, deliver us.

VIVA SAN FERMÍN

FOUR WEEKS AGO, glancing at the front page of the *New York Times*, I realized it was July 7th—*Siete de Julio*. For nearly sixty years I have regarded that day as one of the most significant of my life. What follows is highly personal and confessional. Don't read further unless you care for that sort of thing. July 7th is the beginning of the fiesta of San Fermín, held in the Saint's honor every year in Pamplona, Spain. (Ernest Hemingway's 1926 novel *The Sun Also Rises* made the fiesta world-famous.) On that date in 1965 Bob Call, my friend and fellow priest, during our summer vacations from our New Jersey parishes, entered into this week-long fiesta, determined to do our best to have a complete Pamplonican experience. Dressed in "mufti"—civilian clothes—with red *pañuelos* around our necks, we were disguised as normal persons. Our time there turned out to be, at least for an innocent like me, life-altering. That week merited a crucial chapter in my 2007 memoir, *Belief*. The first 200 pages of that book explain my 15-year battle with doubts about the existence of God, a struggle that had ended in 1964 with my mind finally and quietly embracing atheism. But I still believed in the Catholic Church's social mission, as in my parish work of teaching, running athletic programs, counseling parishioners, presiding over weddings, etc. Additionally, I still carried with me the remnants of years of repression and unworldliness associated with being a Catholic cleric. Although by now an unbeliever, I was still tied emotionally to the

Church. But Pamplona, with surprising quickness, accelerated the undoing of those ties.

Bob Call and I quickly situated ourselves in Pamplona's Plaza del Castillo, the center of the fiesta and our home base for the coming week. The Plaza, a large square, offering plenty of grass and trees, paths and benches, along with a bandstand and an area for dancing, was surrounded by three huge cafés, the Iruña, the Choko, and the Bearin. Our taking part in that fiesta happened nearly 60 years ago, but the experience remains to me as vivid as ever. I set down here a précis, some of it borrowed from the more elaborate account in my memoir.

Noon struck, a skyrocket went up, and the fiesta exploded. Everybody started shouting and clapping and dancing to music that came at you from all directions—from military bands, fife bands, string bands, and the ever-present *peñas,* or young men's athletic clubs, each with its own street band. The party had begun. We purchased *botas,* wineskins with straps that were hung about one's neck; everybody had a *bota* and offered a drink (a squirt) to everyone they met. A wild, yet controlled and hard-to-explain excitement and happiness prevailed.

At nightfall, in the Plaza, we watched fireworks. Debris and ashes floated down on everyone. Nobody cared. Delirium was general, and we were part of it, and, for all I know, it meant more to us, more to me for certain, than to most others. Because in my case (Call's too) this was happening to a priest. As a priest, I had been to parties, and had on occasion had slightly more to drink than was good for me. But Pamplona was different. This party, with its call for a surrender of inhibitions and restraints, was going to last for eight days. (The drinking, wine only, was spread out, tempered; people did not become intoxicated, simply happy.) The priesthood, to which I had dedicated myself for sixteen years, boy and man, seemed far away, much farther than the 3,500 miles to Paterson, New Jersey. No one had the slightest suspicion that I was a priest. I was posing as an ordinary person, allowing myself to slip unnoticed into this sensuous and pagan scene. I was venturing into a week-long *dies non*, a time when no rules obtained. My religious ties, as I have said, were loosening.

Each day of the fiesta revolved around two events, the encierro and the bullfight. At six-thirty the next morning we were among those who got up, or those who had not gone to bed, to witness the encierro or running of the bulls through the town streets to the bull ring. It was exciting, dangerous for the runners, and quickly over. The bull fights themselves began at five in the afternoon. Call had gotten us good tickets, *sombra*, or shaded seats. That we were priests, something known only to ourselves, added to the daring, the edge of our attending this mysterious ritual. The bull fight, reprehensible in many ways, nevertheless captivated me.

After the first full day the fiesta became blurred almost as it was happening. I experienced it as a jangled maze of early-morning encierros and late-afternoon bullfights, of tilted *botas* and *porrónes* of red wine; of bars that laid out trays of *bocadillos* of hard-boiled eggs in olive oil and chunks of salami and bread and served glasses of Fundador brandy for about a dime. But mostly there come back to me nights at the Café Iruña, nights alive with wine and the music of wandering *peñas*. I remember a rocket that hit a balcony, a celebrating French soccer team that had just won some championship cup, a young woman who accompanied them but wandered from table to table making conversation, a German motorcyclist arrested and thrown into jail overnight for arguing about a parking spot. I recall promising to send a book to a Spanish girl. Call and I would sit late into the night at this western side of the square, drinking and talking, as the three big cafés slowly emptied out, and groups of survivors came together to form new, fleeting friendships at 3 am.

It went on like this for days. People got tired and clothes became dirty. The Fiesta of San Fermín looked worn. By the sixth day I wanted a break. I told Call I was taking the car for a day and a night to San Sebastian. On the beach there, I spread my towel in the sand near three young women and lay down and began reading a recent *New Yorker*. Should I, still in a Pamplonican mood, approach them? Go up to these girls (as all young women were called in 1965) in what amounted to flirting? It took a lot of nerve on my part. I had never done such a thing, but it was amazingly easy:

> "Hello there," I said, "are you from the States?" The words sounded conventional and silly.
> "From California. We thought you were English."
> "No, I'm from New Jersey. A schoolteacher." (I did teach in St Mary's High.)

Their names were Fay, Nina, and Linda. I thought them attractive, especially Linda, the shortest of the three, who had a pretty, roundish, dimpled face. She wore a red bikini. The girls had never heard of Pamplona, and I did my best to explain it to them; eventually my listeners were persuaded that it would be a shame to have come this close to Pamplona at this time and to miss the celebration. They accepted my offer to drive them there the next day, the last of the fiesta.

That night we four went to dinner. Here I was, on the first "date" in my life, and clumsily enough, I had three girls. Afterwards, I guided them to a Flamenco bar near the boardwalk and thence to a dance place with American music. While Fay and Nina danced, Linda and I danced, or rather I did my poor best to follow. Our performance seemed to amuse people–the other dancers, the waiters, the band. I explained to her that I was a terrible dancer, but she didn't seem to mind that I was such a klutz. The next song was a slow number. She danced close. She was wearing an orange silk sleeveless dress, and her smooth bare arms were perfectly tanned and alluring. I kept asking myself if I were really here, in San Sebastian, Spain, dancing slowly, even romantically, with a beautiful young woman. She interrupted my reverie by asking "And what did you think of my bikini today?" "Well," I said with a laugh, "I thought it was swell." "They have to fit just right, you know. That's the secret." "Yes, I suppose so. Or that's part of the secret," I added gallantly.

The next day I drove the three young women to Pamplona and got them and their luggage into the Hotel de los Tres Reyes, a great contrast to the cold-water flat where Call and I were staying. I engaged with the concierge for three extra tickets to the last of the bullfights. The girls were to meet up with Call and me at the Café Iruña at 4 pm. By the time they arrived they already loved the fiesta and had supplied themselves with red *pañuelos*.

Halfway through the bullfights, sitting in the shade section with Linda—we had separated ourselves from the others—I realized I was trying to explain too much. I had described everything from the procession and the permission to the little colored ribbons on the bull's neck indicating the farm that bred him. Then I stopped and quit playing the apologist, omitting all mention of boxing, the Chicago slaughterhouses, the Spanish temperament, or–God help us–anything about life and death drama. Antonio Ordóñez (the son of the matador who had been the original for Hemingway's Pedro Romero in *The Sun Also Rises)* gave such a performance with the final bull as to provide a storybook ending to that part of the fiesta.

Call and I took our three "girls" to the Rey Noble, one of the best restaurants in the city, where we had gazpacho, paella, and white wine. Later we went to the Plaza and sat on the ground against some trees and watched the last of the fireworks. The fiesta was bubbling over even as it was phasing out. We tried to dance but this was impossible in the crowd. Instead, we talked and drank. It was past two in the morning when Call and I walked the young women back to their hotel, where we said goodnight.

"We don't know how to thank you," Linda said. "It's been the best day of our trip."

"Thank you," I said, "Our pleasure."

That was it. Our three friends were to be off early the next morning by train to Barcelona. Between my favorite, Linda, and me there had not been even one mild embrace, much less a kiss. But these young women, conjoined to the exuberance of the fiesta, had helped transform me, and a bit more slowly, Bob Call. (Many years later I told one of his daughters, on her wedding day, that she had me to thank for the whole business, me and that car ride to San Sebastian.) I like to think that later in 1965 three young women back in California told their friends of the man from New Jersey that they had met on the beach at San Sebastian, and how he taken them to dinner and then driven them in his car to an amazing festival at Pamplona; and about how, once there, he and his friend had escorted them to cafés, bullfights, a beautiful restaurant, fireworks; and also how these two entertaining young men—I like to think they saw us this way—had simply wanted to share with them the delights of San Fermín, how neither of them made any sexual advance, untoward or otherwise. A short, chance episode, diverting but soon enough forgotten and of no importance to them. Little did they know just how big an adventure that casual encounter had been for me. I had begun to learn a lesson that most people did not need to learn, namely a release from religious bonds and inhibitions. I had still to discover how fully to enjoy "the good things of the earth," but I had made a start. That this was happening to me at the age of 32 made it all the more thrilling.

There, I've told it. A brief sequel: I went back to St Mary's, Paterson, and enjoyed especially my work in the small parish high school. My next summer vacation, 1966, was spent, again in mufti, in Greenwich Village, in a dark, shabby–bathtub in the kitchen– railway apartment. I was again posing as a normal person, this time as a somewhat bohemian would-be writer. (I produced an account of the previous year's Pamplona festival, published in an obscure little magazine ten years later.) For the fun of it, two evenings a week, I took a Continuing Education course (20th Century Literature) at NYU. In that class I met Marianne Gsell and told her about the glories of Pamplona. Why not a little fiesta of our own? A year later I left Paterson and the priesthood.

The following year Marianne and I were married. Viva San Fermín.

CHILD ABUSE

WE ALL KNOW horrific stories of physical abuse of children by priests in this country: scores of thousands of reported cases and even more unreported cases, this enormity coupled with the criminal cover-up by the bishops. This moral bankruptcy was followed by the financial bankruptcy of many dioceses. The generous millions of dollars donated by the faithful on Sunday mornings went to compensate victims and to defend bishops accused of the crime of abetting pederasts. I could relate numerous stories told to me: of a priest insisting on holding a boy's penis as he gave him absolution in a private confession; of a priest visiting a family and, under color of hearing confessions in the bedroom, proceeding to make the sign of the cross with his fingers on the bared breasts of a 14-year-old girl; of a pastor discovered by a fellow curate in bed with an altar boy. But such stories being by now notorious and at the same time old news, my focus here is on psychological but equally real child abuse. (Richard Dawkins asserts that teaching children to believe in God is child abuse, a radical view to be sure; that religion teaches children to believe in superstition is more easily substantiated.) In this third and concluding blog on the Roman Catholic Church and sex, I put forth this thesis: the Church's teaching on sex amounted to and still amounts to child abuse.

How to prove that those teachings were child abuse? How does one prove the obvious? With people unwilling to look the evidence squarely in the face, it's just about impossible. That the insane teachings of the Church were wrong, no sane person can deny. For example, the tenet that taking mental pleasure in thoughts about anything sexual—not just sexual acts, but mental pictures of, say, bikini-clad women—was a mortal sin that merited burning in hell forever. Did the inculcating of such fantastic and horrible doctrines to the credulous young amount to child sexual abuse? The answer should be an obvious yes, and I'll set down in evidence a handful of instances from my own family.

My dear mother was a smart, loving, generous, fully engaged, and wonderful parent. But part of her life was spoiled by her Catholic upbringing, notably eight years in a Catholic grade school. St Nicholas in Jersey City was run by old-world German nuns. My mother's sister recounted to me an incident illustrative of just how wacky the nuns there were when it came to anything concerning sex. Two neighbors of theirs, both eighth graders, Emil and Frances, were friends, and Emil—the smartest boy in the school—was reported to have carried Frances' books home from school. He was immediately expelled, just short of graduation. You can extrapolate from this what the instruction was like at St Nicholas school.

Beyond her years at St Nicholas, my mother had no other schooling, and all her life she carried with her a reticence about anything even remotely connected with sex. She could never, for example, say a word to me about "the facts of life" (my father, not a cradle Catholic and therefore less puritanical, would have considered such lessons a woman's job. Where my parents thought I would learn about sex I have no idea.) Only once did my mother explain one of the mysteries to me. I was living in a house with her and my two sisters, the elder sister being now a teenager, and she felt obliged to tell me about menstruation. She managed to soften the blow by stressing that it was natural, that all women and female animals had monthly periods of blood flow, even the squirrels outside the kitchen window where we sat during this painful lesson. (To this day I am not sure about squirrels, but I thought it was a nice touch). But at the time even my young self realized how difficult this necessary instruction was for her. I was almost compelled to say, "That's Okay, Mom. You told it. Now relax." My mother, so perfectly common sensical in everything else, was "off" on sex. She became upset with my 17-year-old sister Audrey because she had met up with friends in the house of a girlfriend whose parents were away. A few boys had been there! My mother could not even talk of "bathroom stuff" with us. I recall a phone conversation when she told me that my younger sister—who was 24 at the time—had for medical reasons to bring "something in a bottle" for lab work at a hospital. Where did this otherwise sensible, down-to-earth woman get these ridiculous inhibitions? We know damn well.

How about the next generation? How about me? I was psychologically abused, for sure. The distressing side of religion arrived in 1945, when I was 12, in the person of the Reverend Edward J. Scully, who became the pastor of our rural parish. Scully was a devoted, earnest man of God, but also deeply conservative, puritanical, sex-obsessed, woman-fearing, and deep down, woman-hating. You might say he arrived at the same time as did my adolescence, and he moved right in on me, the only son in one of the few Catholic families in that part of his parish. No matter what you confessed, he wanted to know if you had had "impure thoughts," and he always asked me and other young boys about masturbation, even when we didn't know what he was talking about. He came to mold and form my Catholicism, the morality of which revolved around "holy purity." It was Scully who, in the confessional, explained to me the facts of life, so that I would know what it was I was especially not supposed to think about. Even worse than the mortal sins of "impure thoughts" was kissing while playing games like "Post Office" at Boy Scout parties. Such sins had to be confessed to him, the only priest available. Moreover, to hide a mortal sin in confession, to "make a bad confession," was itself an even worse sin, the whole business cascading into a morass of guilt and worry. Junior High School parties and dances disturbed me terribly. Scully had me always on the rack: dancing was not in itself absolutely sinful but did constitute an "occasion of sin," and to place oneself in an occasion of serious sin was itself a mortal sin. Embracing a girl and, as I have said, kissing, except such kisses as one might give one's mother, was gravely sinful, no mitigating circumstances allowed. He even held up the example of St Aloysius, who would not look at his own mother for fear of sin.

Things got worse when my mother insisted that after graduation from the ninth grade I transfer to a Catholic high school. There, at a three-day retreat, I resolved to become a priest, with Scully as my spiritual advisor. By him I was launched upon a completely girl-free "pure" life. The focus on avoiding impure sexual thoughts dogged me for about four years and nearly drove me to a nervous breakdown. I got away from Scully, regained my equilibrium, and went on to become a reasonably sensible seminarian and parish priest. But I was, in fact, a survivor. I had been abused.

The third generation? If it took me years to wake up, not so for one of my nieces, the eldest daughter of my sister Audrey. Karen relates how she, at about age 12 and in the sixth grade, told the parish priest in confession that she had talked about "impure things" (boys) with a girlfriend; the priest insisted on knowing who the girlfriend was (this in a small Catholic school) and told Karen that she must never again have anything to do with that girl. Karen pleaded in vain that the girl was her best friend. Nothing doing. The prohibition was absolute. The friend must be avoided if Karen were to be forgiven her grievous sin. But Karen decided, while saying her penance, that she would go ahead and remain in this "sinful" friendship. Brave little girl. What to think of this priest? The term "sick bastard" leaps to mind.

There is no gainsaying the fact—for those of us who still believe in facts—that the ordinary sexual instruction which the Roman Catholic Church inflicted on the young should be labelled, *literally*, child abuse. It was "only" psychological, but only a fool would deny its real harm.

METAPHOR EVERYWHERE

I WAS SPEAKING metaphorically." You certainly were. We all speak metaphorically, all the time. Marshall McLuhan went so far as to say that every word in every language is a metaphor, but that was a stretch—unless he was speaking metaphorically. Metaphor is an enormous subject. Your average person in the street knows that metaphor is an implied comparison, "He was a wet blanket at the party," and that metaphor is closely related to simile, an expressed comparison, "He came in looking like an unmade bed." Both metaphor and simile carry the warning not to mix them: "On the dance floor he was a monkey riding a bicycle with two left feet." And it's good to keep in mind that any part of speech can be a metaphor. Noun: "Their house was a three-ring circus." Adjective: "That was a tasteless remark." Verb: "He murdered that song." Adverb: "She footstamplingly dashed off a harsh letter" (almost a simile, because ly is rooted in like). Even prepositions qualify: "She's into classical music; he's on drugs." We love metaphors, they enliven our speech, and we embrace them because the straightforward way of putting things just doesn't always come up to snuff, doesn't bring home what we are trying to say. I quote Doctor Johnson: "Sir, as for metaphorical expression, that is a great excellence in style, when it is used with propriety, for it gives you two ideas for one;—conveys the meaning more luminously, and generally with a perception of delight." We are up to our ears in metaphors; we can hardly open our mouths without using one. What percentage of our everyday language is metaphor? Beats me. I don't have even a ballpark figure. But we continually speak in metaphors, and some are more obviously metaphoric than others:

> He's the top banana.
> You're the cream in my coffee.
> Tom's mother says he is her sun, moon, and star.
> His career seemed to be going south.
> She starred in the movie; his star was setting.
> Our time together was not exactly heaven on earth.

Others are more subtly metaphoric:

> I looked after her dog.
> She nailed that song.
> The market collapsed.
> She's deep into flamenco.
> I'll catch the A train.
> His insolence floored me.

We talk like that, don't we? And we are awash in vulgar metaphors:

> Shit happens.
> Charlie's a real son of a bitch.
> You piece of crap!
> We were just farting around.
> My life is fucked up.
> Who the fuck are you?

Ordinary and unexciting examples, these. But great literature, especially poetry, fairly oozes with original metaphors and similes: Homer's "rosy-fingered dawn"; the Psalmist's "The Lord is my Shepherd"; Shakespeare's England as "This royal throne of kings, this sceptered isle … this seat of Mars, This other Eden, demi-paradise, This fortress built by Nature … this little world, This precious stone set in the silver sea…" In fact, any good poet can surprise us with innovative metaphors. Any? Take Philip Larkin, for example, a poet I happen to be reading these days. (He was in many ways a less than admirable person, but the problem of separating the art from the artist is not part of this discussion.) Larkin is given to straightforward everyday speech with or without metaphors:

> Sexual intercourse began
> In nineteen sixty-three
> (Which was rather late for me)—
> Between the end of the *Chatterley* ban
> And the Beatles' first LP.

Or, "Get stewed: Books are a load of crap"; and, famously, "They fuck you up, your mum and dad." But when Larkin does reach for an unfamiliar metaphor or simile, the result can be striking: Light from the sun "bathes the *serene foreheads* of houses"; a thrush is singing in the garden and "*astonishing* the brickwork"; hoping for good things, we watch "*the tiny, sparkling armada of promises* draw near"; "The bells *discuss* the hour's gradations"; Sidney Bechet's long-held note on a soprano sax falls on the listener "as they say love should, *like an enormous yes*." (borrowed from Joyce's Molly Bloom?). *Aubade*, the poet's just-before-dawn meditation on "*unresting* death," that "*anaesthetic* from which none come round," describes his dread of death as raging out "in *furnace* fear" and standing in his mind as "*plain as a wardrobe*" in a room; this is a fear which "no trick," certainly not religion, "*that vast moth-eaten musical brocade*," can dispel. But life goes on: "Meanwhile telephones *crouch*, getting ready to ring in locked-up offices, and all the *uncaring* intricate *rented* world begins to rouse."

Among contemporary *prose* writers, Edward St Aubyn's Patrick Melrose novels overflow with original metaphors and similes. We read of old "*claret-stained* anecdotes"; of someone glimpsing "the pink flowers of a magnolia *protesting* against the black and white half-timbered façade"; of a constant complainer who "had to *bail out the flooding dinghy* of her discontent." Patrick learns of an inheritance: "*The long arm* of his great grandfather … was going to *pluck* him out of his [relative poverty]" because his ancestor's candle factory distilled cheap greases that "were still *lubricating* the life of one of his descendants"; a character says, "I mean, if it's true, reincarnation is *like having Alzheimer's on a huge scale*"; Patrick's mother, to get time away from her murderous husband, flees to her car which was "*like a consulate in a strange city*"; at her funeral Patrick "patted the coffin, *as an owner might pat a winning racehorse.*"

These examples demonstrate how almost all metaphors use ordinary language in unusual contexts. In this essay with its hundred or so metaphors, only two, the words "footstampingly" and, more happily, "rosy-fingered," are attention-grabbing in themselves.

For further insight into metaphors, I consult that ancient authority, Henry Fowler. His 100-year-old but still useful article begins: "Our vocabulary is largely built on metaphors; we use them, though perhaps not consciously, whenever we speak or write." We already knew that. But then he goes on to distinguish "live" and "dead" metaphors; to list the "pitfalls" connected with them; and to investigate our "self-consciousness" about mixed metaphors. Here's a quick summary with a few modest thoughts of my own and some up-to-date examples.

Live and dead metaphors: Live metaphors are those we are conscious of as taking the place of literal equivalents: "She is a *walking encyclopedia*." "Trump *threw his lawyer under the bus*." More common are dead metaphors, i.e., words or phrases dead *as metaphors*, those that have been used so often that speaker and hearer alike are unaware that the words are not to be taken literally. We say, "His jokes *kill* me" and "I'm *dying* to see you." Fowler's illustration plays with the word *sift*: "The men were *sifting* meal" is literal. "Satan will *sift* you as wheat" is a live metaphor. "We will *sift* the evidence" is a "half dead" or maybe "three-quarters dead" metaphor, because people do not recognize *sift* as a metaphor for *examine* (and *examine* itself, Fowler informs us, is in turn a long dead metaphor for *weigh*). Indeed, it is often hard to draw the line between live and dead metaphors. (And, yes, dead metaphors are often the dictionary's secondary definitions; and good metaphors often become clichés.) Note too that any consideration of metaphors, dead or live, reminds us that context creates metaphors, renders speech metaphorical or literal: "He's not exactly an altar-boy" can describe either a lad who works in the church but does not serve at Mass, or someone who is a young delinquent; "Don't make me laugh" can mean that your talk makes my broken ribs hurt or that you should stop bullshitting me.

Under "pitfalls" Fowler lists five kinds of failed metaphor: unsustained, overdone, spoilt, battling, and (our old friend) mixed.

Unsustained metaphors are those that "don't work": "He was still in the middle of those 20 years of neglect which only began to *lift* in 1950." Fowler comments that the "plunge into metaphor at *lift*, which presupposes a mist, is too sudden after the literal 20 years of neglect; years do not lift."

Overdone metaphors are extended metaphors stretched too far: "The *long arm of coincidence rolled up its sleeves* and *set to work* with a rapidity and vigour which defy description." Extended metaphors can be miraculously good but only in the hands of someone who knows what he is doing, as in the almost-all-too-familiar "All the world's a stage" with ourselves as "players" of many "parts", in "acts" comprising seven ages, etc.

Spoilt metaphors are live metaphors rendered incongruous by context: "We must not allow ourselves to be *stampeded* into stagnation."

Battling metaphors are dead metaphors that do not "lie together" nicely: "It seems impossible to *crush* the Republican Senate's *aim* to forestall the bill." *Crush* for *defeat* and *aim* for *purpose* are good dead metaphors, but they clash. Fowler says that you cannot crush an aim. He adds that much of the misuse of metaphors (especially dead ones) amounts to "tasteless word selection."

Mixed metaphors, those against which we are constantly being warned, are live metaphors that collide. They are easily detected: "In this debate we should not *throw in the sponge* when the enemy is already *on the run*." By contrast, two dead metaphors can readily be mixed: "She has an *upbeat, sunny* disposition." Moreover, a live metaphor can be tidily combined with a dead one because we don't recognize the dead one as a metaphor: "You *drive me crazy* with your talk about the two *bookends* to your argument." But, to repeat, we must avoid live metaphors that don't "mix," as in "Forget about your *old flame* because there are plenty of *fish in the sea*." I fear St Aubyn goes astray when he writes that a character "had experienced a late-adolescent *crush* on the History of Art, rudely *guillotined* by her disinheritance." But how about the most quoted lines in the language, whether "to suffer the slings and arrows of outrageous fortune, Or to take arms against a sea of troubles"? Sounds mixed? No problem. It's Shakespeare, fircrissakes.

Fowler says that "self-consciousness" about mixing metaphors prompts writers to delight in accusing each other of having done so or in announcing that they themselves are about to do so: "The offence apparently [is] not to mix metaphors but to be unaware that you have done it." He notes that to *change* metaphors is not the same as to *mix* them: "A writer may change his metaphors as often as he likes ... but he should not have to ask leave to do it; if the result is bad, his apology will not mend matters; and if the change is not bad, then no apology is called for." Thus, I think Fowler would give the green light to "Joe's quick temper was his Achilles heel, the chink in his armor, his one weak spot." Or, to look to a master, consider this stanza from W H Auden on the death of a lover:

> He was my North, my South, my East and West,
>   My working week, and my Sunday rest,
>   My noon, my midnight, my talk, my song;
>   I thought that love would last forever: I was wrong.

To tumble from the heights back down to Earth: we are "allowed" to mix metaphors as a joke. I know a writer who tried to be funny in a lengthy sentence that went something like this: "If as writers we want to keep our house in order and not fall asleep at the switch, if we don't want to be up the creek with no light at the end of the tunnel, if we don't want to telegraph our ignorance of the heaven-sent rules of style, we must embrace and focus our vigilance against mixing metaphors." Not very funny. But a comic genius can use metaphors to good effect. James Thurber, in "The Secret Life of James Thurber," writes of how the mental picturings of his childhood deeply troubled him. (His were so different, Thurber tells us, from Salvador Dali's, which included biting sick bats, kicking a dead horse, pushing a tiny playmate off a bridge, caressing a crutch.) The worries Thurber had as a child resulted from taking adult metaphors literally and imagining them: the man who left town "under a cloud"; the woman who "was all cut up" after her daughter's unsuccessful surgery; the person on the other end of a phone conversation who claimed to be "all ears"; the husband "who couldn't put his foot down"; the lady who was "always up in the air"; the man who "lost his head during a fire"; his little cousin who was "crying her heart out."

So, all that said, what is the best metaphor ever coined—*coined*? That's a walk, a cinch. No, it's not "All the world's a stage" or "You are my sunshine." It's Darwin's world-shaking and original phrase, "natural selection."